Evaluation of Instruction in Individually Guided Education

Evaluation of Instruction in Individually Guided Education

William Wiersma
Stephen G. Jurs
University of Toledo

Addison-Wesley Publishing Company
Reading, Massachusetts • Menlo Park, California
London • Amsterdam • Don Mills, Ontario • Sydney

This book and the correlated films and filmstrips are in the
Leadership Series in Individually Guided Education,
Herbert J. Klausmeier, Editor.
Development of this series was funded by
The Sears-Roebuck Foundation.

ISBN 0-201-19211-X
ABCDEFGHIJ-AL-79876

Editor's Foreword

These are exciting and challenging times in American education. Personnel in local school districts, intermediate education agencies, state education agencies, and teacher education institutions are cooperating as never before to improve the quality of education for children, high school youth, and college students. Bringing Individually Guided Education, a new approach in education, to an ever increasing number of students provides the focus for many of these cooperative efforts. This Leadership Series in Individually Guided Education is designed to help teacher educators and other educational leaders in their improvement efforts. It comprises ten sets of printed materials and correlated films and filmstrips. The materials have been developed for use both in credit courses offered on college campuses and in local schools and in noncredit staff development programs carried out in the local schools.

The set of materials for Evaluation of Instruction in Individually Guided Education consists of this textbook and an accompanying instructor's guide which provides aids to instructors for meeting the needs of their students in their particular situations. Several films and filmstrips of the Series may also be used with this textbook and guide.

The authors of this book, William Wiersma and Stephen G. Jurs, are scholars in the field of measurement, research design, and evaluation. They have contributed to the development of the performance-based teacher education program in IGE at the University of Toledo and have assisted local schools in solving problems of measurement and evaluation.

I have enjoyed the cooperative and productive working relationships with these scholars, the film producers, the publisher, and others in developing this comprehensive set of multimedia materials. To assure that the users of this and other sets of materials in the Leadership Series get attractive, high quality, usable materials and also are not presented with conflicting interpretations of IGE in either the books or the visuals, I personally reviewed each book from its first chapter outline, through its several field-tested drafts, and the final manuscript. I did the same for each visual from the initial content outline, through the several drafts of the script, rough cuts, and fine cuts. Many other persons also participated in the production, review, and quality control process.

In this regard I am pleased to recognize the many school personnel, state education agency personnel, professors, and students who participated in field tests and review sessions; the consultants with expertise in the various subject matter fields or in the filmic quality and instructional effectiveness of the visuals; Anthony E. Conte, James M. Lipham, Wesley C. Meierhenry, and William Wiersma for serving on the Project Publications Board; Judith Amacker, William R. Bush, James R. Dumpson, Martin W. Essex, Nancy Evers, Lovelia P. Flournoy, John R. Palmer, Edward C. Pomeroy, Richard A. Rossmiller, B. Othanel Smith, Lorraine Sullivan, and James Swinney for serving on the Project Advisory Committee; Leslie C. Bernal, G. R. Bowers, Eleanor Buehrig, Xavier Del Buono, Lee M. Ellwood, G. W. Ford, Marvin J. Fruth, George Glasrud, James Hixson, Ronald Horn, Terry Jackson, L. Wayne Krula, Max Poole, Kenneth B. Smith, James Stoltenberg, Michael F. Tobin, Philip Vik, James E. Walter, S. Edward Weinswig, and William Wiersma for serving on the Project Steering Committee. Particular recognition is given to the members of minority groups who reviewed the visuals so as to avoid having any racism or sexism appear in them. Special thanks are merited by the dedicated staff of the IGE Teacher Education Project: L. Joseph Lins, Project Administrator; Mary Melvin, Project Assistant to the Director; Marilyn Zoroya, Administrative Specialist and Newsletter Editor, *Teacher Educators IGE Report;* Mary Baban, Donald Granger, and Linda Blanchard, Project Specialists, IGE School Practices; and Arlene Knudsen, my administrative secretary.

The development of these materials became possible through a grant made by The Sears-Roebuck Foundation in 1973 to the IGE Teacher Education Project at The University of Wisconsin—Madison. The authors, editor, and others associated with the Project receive no royalties from the sale of these materials. However, the royalties that accrue will be returned to The University of Wisconsin—Madison to support continuing research, development, and implementation activities related to Individually Guided Education.

Herbert J. Klausmeier
Series Editor and Director
IGE Teacher Education Project
The University of Wisconsin—Madison

Preface

This text emphasizes the practical application of evaluation procedures. Its primary orientation is toward the elementary level and toward programming instruction for the individual student. The content is relevant to the preparation of preservice teacher education students and inservice teachers. In the latter case, the text is relevant to any inservice courses that deal with the evaluation of instruction, or it could be used as a "handbook" by practicing teachers.

The text is not primarily a measurement text, certainly not in the traditional sense. However, it is appropriate for educational measurement and evaluation courses that emphasize practical application. It can serve as a supplementary text in courses preparing prospective and inservice teachers for instruction in Individually Guided Education (IGE). In this way it may be supplementary to the texts used in a curriculum or educational psychology course.

The emphasis within the text is upon the evaluation of student learning. The uses of both teacher-made and published tests are considered. Chapters 1–6 deal with this matter. Chapter 7 discusses the evaluation of instructional programs. Chapter 8 is concerned with reporting student progress.

Examples are used throughout and much of the discussion is directed to "how to do" as well as "a description of" evaluation procedures. At the beginning of each chapter is a statement of chapter objectives for the reader. Discussion topics are presented at the end of each chapter to enhance the reader's understanding of content. References relevant to the content are provided for each chapter.

January 1976   W.W.
University of Toledo   S.J.

Contents

1
Introduction to Measurement and Evaluation

Objectives

After reading this chapter the reader will be able:

- To define measurement, assessment, and evaluation.
- To compare norm-referenced and criterion-referenced interpretations of measurement results.
- To explain why and how evaluation is an essential part of instruction.
- To indicate the groups responsible for evaluation in Individually Guided Education.

Measurement, assessment, and evaluation are essential functions in that they are or should be an integral part of instruction; and it is important that they be conducted in an organized and systematic manner.

While measurement, assessment, and evaluation are important for all schools, they are crucial when using the instructional programming model (IPM) of individually guided education (IGE).* IGE emphasizes meeting the needs of individual students and in order to do this there must be assessment of student characteristics both before and after instruction. Moreover, each teacher within the Instruction and Research Unit (the basic instructional unit in IGE) must understand the application of measurement, assessment, and evaluation to the improvement of instruction.

The concepts of measurement, assessment, and evaluation discussed in the next few pages, although applicable to education generally, are related directly to instructional programming for the individual student, a component of IGE. Since instructional programming for the individual student can be implemented in all kinds of schools, the reader should understand the more specific as well as the general applications of the concepts. For that reason examples of the concepts are presented in the context of IGE, especially in the IPM. The IPM lends itself especially well to the application of evaluation procedures.

MEASUREMENT AS QUANTIFICATION

Measurement accompanies a host of activities in our society and involves varying degrees of precision, depending upon the measuring instrument and the uses to be made of the findings. It is relatively easy to understand the measurement of something like the dimensions of the rooms of a school in terms of length and width. Having an adequate yardstick readily makes such measurement possible. It is, however, much more difficult to conceptualize and operationalize the measurement of personality.

Regardless of what is to be measured, or the potential difficulty of such measurement, it is important to obtain a consistent meaning of measurement and terms associated with it. A broad definition of measurement is often given as the assignment of numerals to objects or

---

* It is not the purpose here to provide a detailed discussion of IGE. Parts of texts and entire texts are devoted to such discussions. These are referenced at the end of this chapter. The IPM is provided in Figure 1.1 which appears subsequently in this chapter.

events according to rules. A numeral is a symbol such as 1, 2, 3, ... However, the numeral itself has no relevance to measurement until quantitative meaning is assigned to it. Sometimes numerals are assigned simply for convenience, such as the assignment of numerals to the players of a baseball team. Such assignment may or may not follow a rule, but in any event, it does not comprise measurement.

Measurements involving length, weight, and volume are commonplace and readily understood by most individuals. The quantification in such measurement is quite apparent. It is not as easily understood that measurement of educational attributes such as cognitive performance, intellectual ability, and attitudes involves the same general concepts and ideas. The crucial element is, of course, the rule. It is for this reason that the rule and what goes into it require specific attention. Suppose that a student is measured on science achievement through the use of a twenty-item test, each item representing five points. The rule is that a correct response to an item receives five points and the points are totaled for the achievement score. Even if the rule is applicable and produces a score representing quantification, the test cannot produce measurement relevant to the achievement unless the test items are appropriate. This is somewhat analogous to measuring the length of a room with a tape measure having inconsistent gradations for inches. It is much easier to standardize the length of an inch than the quantitative values of test items, but as long as the rule can be operationally defined, measurement is possible.

Assessment and Testing

The terms assessment and test are quite closely associated with measurement and are not always used with consistent meaning. Although measurement and assessment should not be considered synonymous, they are quite close in meaning. Assessment is considered to be the practical application of measurement, the actual performance of some type of measurement. For example, the administration of a mathematics test or a physical fitness test could be considered assessment. In the latter case, we say that physical fitness is being assessed.

When assessment is taking place information or data are being collected, but we must be careful not to ascribe too broad a meaning to assessment. For example, assessment does not include making judgments about the data, which is reserved for evaluation as we shall see subsequently. We generally do not consider assessment as being a part of measurement theory. Reference is not made to a theory of assessment, for example.

Test, on the other hand, has a narrower meaning than either

measurement or assessment. Test most commonly refers to a set of items or questions, designed to be presented to one or more students under specified conditions. When giving a test, assessment takes place, but all assessment is not necessarily testing. For example, suppose a teacher were recording information about the learning styles preferred by a student. This would be an example of assessment, but we would not consider it testing. Testing is, of course, the process of administering a test, and in this sense testing is subsumed under assessment. The test is the stimulus to which the response is made. Tests are not limited to paper and-pencil inventories. We may have oral tests for communication skills and performance tests for psychomotor skills.

In summarizing the relationships of the terms test, assessment, and measurement, using the definitions above, we see that all testing is subsumed under assessment, and all assessment is subsumed under measurement. In fact, when actually collecting data, measurement and assessment are the same, and if a test is used for the data collection, then the assessment is being conducted through testing.

EVALUATION FOR DECISION MAKING

Teachers who attempt to individualize instruction are in a continual process of making instructional decisions. There are basically two kinds of instructional decisions. These decisions relate to (1) The performance and progress of individual students, and (2) the effectiveness (or lack of effectiveness) of an individual's instructional programs. The plural use of programs here is important to note. When individualizing instruction, students are in their own programs tailored to their needs. For example, we do not view the mathematics instruction as one broad program, even though a single mathematics text series may be used. Since instruction and assessment take place at the level specific to the student, it is best to consider the instructional programs at that level as well.

On what basis is decision making to take place? Certainly not on a random basis and hopefully ad hoc, intuitive judgments will be used sparingly, if at all. Decision making in IGE should be based on objective information. This brings us to the concept of evaluation.

Any number of specific definitions of educational evaluation has been suggested and most are compatible. For our purposes, we will accept the definition proposed by Stufflebeam (1971, xxv):

> Evaluation is the science of providing information for decision making —the process of delineating, obtaining, and providing useful information for judging decision alternatives.

This definition is broad and involves measurement, assessment, and testing. It has wide application, and the complexity of activities necessary to meet this definition depend upon the specific situation in which evaluation is being conducted. In our meaning of evaluation we will include making the judgment; that is, making the decision.

Evaluation and Instructional Programming for the Individual Student

Evaluation is generally not an end in itself, but a means to effective instruction. In its simplest form we can describe the activities that relate to the evaluation of student learning and related instrucion by the following sequence:

> Develop instructional objectives including the criteria of acceptable performance ──────→ measure performance ──────→ compare the measured performance to the performance indicated by the criteria ──────→ judge the measured performance ──────→ act on judgment (Klausmeier and Goodwin 1975, p. 464).

The sequence above indicates that evaluation is objective-based, a necessary condition of evaluation in IGE. Note that there must be criteria of acceptable performance or achievement. The criteria may be explicitly or implicitly contained in the objective; or statements of objectives may be supplemented with stated criteria. A set of curriculum materials may have some objectives that call for full mastery, others that call only for some progress toward mastery, and still others that call merely for participation in certain activities.

An instructional sequence begins with having clearly stated objectives. Although objectives are essential for instruction, preparing instructional objectives is usually not considered as evaluation activity. Measurement, relating measurement to the criterion, and judging are considered direct evaluation activities, and acting on the judgment is usually considered the consequence of the evaluation activity. The preceding activities are general and apply to evaluation in all domains: cognitive, psychomotor, and affective.

Measurement, Assessment, and Evaluation in the IPM

The model for instructional programming for individual students is presented in Figure 1.1. An inspection of the various steps in the model indicates numerous measurement and assessment activities either explicitly stated or implied.

It should be noted that these activities are relevant to both types of decisions, those pertaining to individual students and those related to their instructional programs. For example, the assessment that takes place to determine whether or not the educational objectives

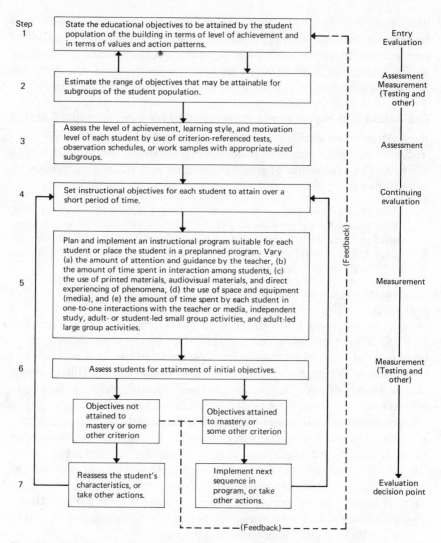

Fig. 1.1 The IPM in IGE with evaluation emphasized at the appropriate steps. Adapted from H. J. Klausmeier, M. R. Quilling, J. S. Sorenson, R. S. Way, and G. R. Glasrud 1971. *Individually guided education and the multiunit school: guidelines for implementation.* Madison, Wisc.: Wisconsin Research and Development Center for Cognitive Learning.

stated in Step 1 of the IPM have been met could relate to a decision on the effectiveness of instructional programs. On the other hand, the measurement of Step 6 directly relates to whether or not individual students have attained their instructional objectives. Of course, the two types of decisions are not independent and there is considerable overlap in the information that applies to the decisions. If large numbers of students fail to meet substantial numbers of their instructional objectives, this information is not only relevant for the individual students, but to the effectiveness of the instructional programming procedures, including the use of materials, methods, equipment, and other elements of instructional programs.

The measurement and assessment activities are specifically indicated on the right side of the figure, and the activities are included in what is basically a continuing evaluation process. The culmination of instructional programming consists of a decision point at which the various decision alternatives that exist must be judged. In order to make appropriate instructional decisions, teachers must have adequate information. Such information is collected and used throughout instructional programming, beginning with the statement of educational objectives and the initial estimate of the range of objectives, through the decision on whether or not objectives have been attained. Thus, the measurement, assessment, and testing become a part of evaluation.

Evaluation is not limited to data collection. In order to complete an instructional sequence for a student or group of students, information must be used for making decisions. In order to make a decision or to have a decision point, two or more decision alternatives must exist. Teachers must make a judgment about the decision alternatives. Instructional decisions play a very important role in individualizing instruction. If some defined course of action were to be followed regardless of the outcomes, there would be no need for evaluation. This should never be the case in IGE.

Types of Evaluation

Writers have coined various terms to distinguish among different types of evaluation. Classification schemes for types of evaluation are, of course, general and have broad application to instructional situations.

One such pair of terms which applies primarily to program evaluation is formative and summative evaluation (Scriven 1967, pp. 39–83). Formative evaluation is the collection and use of data while the instructional program is being developed or implemented. Summative evaluaton is evaluation at the end of an instructional sequence.

An example of the distinction between formative and summative evaluation follows. Suppose an objective-based curriculum program were being implemented. During the implementation of the program, information is being collected and evaluated on matters such as (1) how well the students are attaining the objectives, and (2) the effectiveness of certain kinds of instructional modes relative to students attaining objectives. Suppose that on specific sets of objectives substantial numbers of students are failing to attain the criteria of the objectives. It would hardly be satisfactory to persist through an entire semester or year program under these conditions. Therefore, adjustments would be made during the year in implementing the program. The evaluation might indicate that adjustments in the instructional modes are necessary, or that other sequences of objectives are desirable. It might be that assessment detects an error made in initial placement of a student. A correction should be made immediately. Adjustments of these kinds, made during implementation, are the results of formative evaluation.

On the other hand, summative evaluation is conducted at the conclusion of a period of time such as a semester or year. The entire building staff might evaluate how well a particular curriculum program had been implemented. The student performance on the objectives would be related back to the range of objectives established in Step 2 of the IPM, and even related to the educational objectives of Step 1 of the IPM. At this point an overall evaluation of the particular program is made. This is an example of summative evaluation of an instructional program.

However, the example above of summative evaluation implies a rather long time span and this is not always the case. Suppose a student were working on a portion of an instructional sequence. The objectives and the criteria for attaining the objectives of this sequence are set. Student performance is measured and a judgment made about whether or not the performance meets the criteria. Evaluation is taking place, a decision is being made, and appropriate action will follow. This too is an example of summative evaluation, in this case covering a relatively short time span, possibly only a day or two. Thus, both formative and summative evaluations affect the two kinds of decisions made by unit staff.

Another useful distinction for types of evaluation is process and product evaluation. Evaluation of instructional process, analogous to evaluation of student learning, relates primarily to Steps 3, 4, and 5 of the IPM. If as instruction proceeds it becomes apparent that instructional objectives are not being met, adjustments in the program or the teaching-learning process should be made. Such adjustments are the results of process evaluation. On the other hand, product evaluation relates to instructional products such as curriculum programs, tests, organization, etc.

These types of evaluation—formative, summative, process, product—are not mutually exclusive. For example, formative evaluation can involve (and usually does) both the process of instruction and the products such as curriculum programs. The same is true for summative evaluation. In evaluating an overall set of curriculum materials and procedures we would not limit our consideration merely to how well the student performed. Identifying these types, however, is helpful in understanding evaluation in the instructional setting.

Evaluation and Instructional Objectives

Whether process or product evaluation is being conducted, it is necessary to have relevant information for decision making. Ad hoc data collection with no planning is of little if any use. Evaluation must be related to instructional objectives. Since evaluation is tied so closely to the objectives, an adequate set of instructional objectives is essential for conducting effective evaluation. It is possible, of course, to evaluate observable and measurable effects which occur without being intended. Such effects are important as they relate to the objectives.

Sources of Information

Evaluation information can be obtained from several sources. Certainly, the student is one source, and probably the major source of information—the student's scores on tests, the student's motivation, interests, attitudes, work habits, etc. The home and the community are other potential sources of information. The individual members of the unit staff can also provide useful evaluation information.

Evaluation information must be interpreted in order to be useful. Since the teachers are most closely associated with instruction and most knowledgeable about the data, they are the primary interpreters. Also, teachers are the ones who will be using the information in making judgments and decisions, so they will know what it is they require of the data.

Historically, the approach to interpreting test information has been norm-referenced. This approach has not always been closely tied to instruction, especially individualized instruction. Despite this, there is occasion for norm-referenced measurement and interpretation in IGE. However, in instructional programming for individual students criterion-referenced measurement is more applicable, and the majority of the interpretation is criterion-referenced. Each of these basic approaches to interpretation of data is now discussed. The discussion of norm-referenced interpretations is included primarily as a contrast for criterion-referenced interpretation.

NORM-REFERENCED INTERPRETATIONS

When educators contrast norm-referenced testing (measurement, or assessment) with criterion-referenced testing, they are basically referring to two different ways of interpreting information. An item or a test is neither norm-referenced nor criterion-referenced until an interpretation is made of its score. This concept is analogous to a pitch in baseball. It is neither a ball nor a strike until the umpire makes a call (interpretation).

Norm-referenced interpretation has been historically used in the schools, and this form of interpretation developed from the desire to differentiate among individuals or to discriminate among the individuals of some defined group on whatever is being measured. In norm-referenced measurement an individual's score is interpreted by comparing the score to those of a defined group, often called the normative group. The individual's position in the normative group is of concern, thus the comparison is relative rather than absolute. If a decision is to be made about the position of a student's score relative to the scores of some group, a norm-referenced interpretation is required. This kind of positioning does not specify the performance in absolute terms. Depending upon the norms being used, the same score may be high or it may be low. It is the norm as the basis of comparison that influences the score designation.

Norm-Referenced Interpretation—An Example Using a Standardized Test

Most standardized, achievement tests, especially those covering several skills and academic areas, are primarily designed for norm-referenced interpretations. Norms are generated from the scores of one or more groups of students that have taken the test. Such a group is called the normative group, and in some cases the standardization group. With most standardized tests, the scores of the normative group represent a typical or average performance. The sizes of the normative groups vary considerably for the better known, standardized tests, but generally they tend to be large, in some cases several thousand students.

The Iowa Test of Basic Skills* (ITBS) is a comprehensive test that can be used with grades 1–8. The multilevel edition is intended for use with grades 3–8 and the primary edition for use with the first two grades. The ITBS, multilevel edition, actually consists of 11

---

* The ITBS is published by Houghton Mifflin Company, Boston. Comments in this discussion are based on the *Teacher's Manual,* ITBS by E. F. Lindquist and A. N. Hieronymus, State University of Iowa, 1964.

separate tests covering the basic skills of the elementary school student. Examples of skills covered are Language skills, Study skills, and Mathematics skills, although the majority of the scores are in reading and language arts.

The ITBS Manual provides national percentile norms for grade equivalents for the beginning, middle, and end of the school year. What this means is that a converted score is computed from the raw score. This score is a grade equivalent score, a score that specified the grade and month of grade (based on 10 months) which corresponds with the raw score. For example, if a student's raw score converts to a grade equivalent score of 43 this means that the student's performance is that of a "typical" fourth grader, three months into fourth grade.

The matter of a "typical" fourth grader brings up the concept of norms. What is the performance of a "typical" fourth grader?

It is the performance of the fourth graders in the national sample (consisting of several thousand students) which was used as the normative group. Note that when a student's performance is expressed as a grade equivalent score, it is being compared to the performance of some group, the normative group.

It was mentioned above that national percentile norms are provided for the grades. This simply means that a raw score can be converted to a percentile score which indicates that that percentage of the normative group scored below the given raw score. For example, suppose a fifth grader's raw score converts to a percentile score of 81. This means that 81 percent of the fifth graders in the normative group scored below this particular fifth grader.

In order to illustrate the interpretation of a student's scores on the ITBS, an example of a Pupil Profile Chart is provided in Figure 1.2. Note that there is a total of 15 scores with individual skills and composite test scores. The example happens to include two midyear testings of the same student one year apart. Since the student was in the fourth and fifth grades for the two testings, typical grade equivalent performance would be 45 and 55.

Consider the grade 4 testing. In vocabulary the student was at 46, in reading comprehension at 44, and in arithmetic concepts considerably below grade level at 33. This means that the student was about at typical performance on the first two tests, but performed as did a third grader (in the third month) of the normative group. All scores are interpreted in like manner, referencing them to the performance of the normative group.

The profile charts of the ITBS can be used to plot pupil growth over specified periods. This was done in the example for the period of

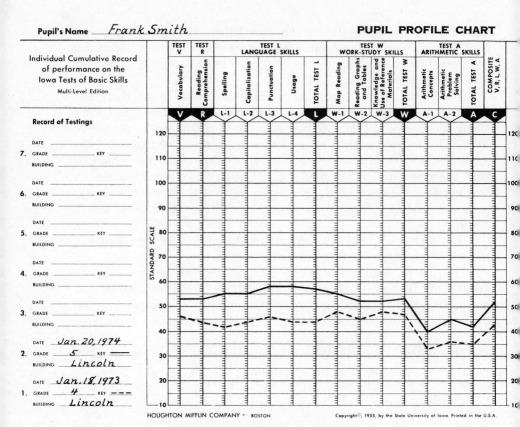

Fig. 1.2 An example Pupil Profile Chart from the ITBS, Boston: Houghton Mifflin. Copyright 1955 by the State University of Iowa.

one year. With norms given for beginning, middle, and end of the school year, the testing schedule can be quite flexible. The results of this kind of norm-referenced testing have been used for diagnostic purposes, indicating in what skills students are below their expected grade levels. But whatever the use, all interpretations are based on the performance of the normative group.

Use of Norm-referenced Tests and Instructional Programming for Individual Students

On the surface, it would seem that there is little, if any, place for norm-referenced assessment in objectives-based, individualized instruction.

After specifying objectives for individual students, the major concern of instructional evaluation is to determine whether or not the student has mastered the objectives. However, many school systems have systemwide testing programs which utilize standardized tests such as the ITBS.

The information from such tests can be helpful to the school in establishing realistic educational objectives and may contribute to the entry evaluation indicated in Figure 1.1.

A norm-referenced source such as the Pupil Profile Chart may provide some information if the test content reflects the instructional objectives. But in itself the test results do not provide enough information for decision making. For example, a misuse of the profile in Figure 1.2 would be to group Frank Smith with students slow in mathematics. It may be that the test does not cover the mathematics objectives set for Frank Smith. The profile does not provide data about factors such as Frank Smith's learning style, nor about his orientation to this kind of a paper-and-pencil test. A serious misuse of this information would be the improper categorization of Frank Smith, for example, as slow in learning mathematics.

Another common misuse of norms found in elementary schools is indicating some type of average as a universally desirable attainment level or standard. Norms were not intended for this purpose and using them in this way is also in conflict with concepts of individualization. For example, if results indicated that the students of the school generally had performed below grade level, it would be improper to set as a goal bringing all students up to grade level. Regardless of whether or not the test reflects the instructional objectives, using the norm as a standard is not appropriate.

The common misuses of normative information can be listed as:

1. Assuming the test content to be an indicator of the instructional objectives when in fact it is not.

2. Using normative information by itself in categorizing students.

3. Setting the norm as some type of standard to be attained by all students.

Data from norm-referenced tests may provide some information for decision making in IGE if the test content reflects the objectives. The Instructional Improvement Committee (IIC) could use such data in setting realistic educational objectives, ones that can be attained, given the student and school characteristics. Individual profiles such as those obtained with ITBS could be made available to the unit staff and used for diagnostic purposes. This is assuming that the objectives of instruction are consistent with whatever the test measures.

One final comment on using standardized, norm-referenced tests. When measuring attitudes, interests, and aptitudes, it would be practically impossible to interpret the results without comparing them to a reference group. The reference groups in such cases are usually typical students, or students with high interest in certain areas, for example. Teachers have no basis for anticipating certain scores, and therefore in order to ascribe meaning to a score, the referent group must be used. For example, a score such as 80 on an interest inventory has no meaning in itself. On the other hand, if the score of 80 is the typical response by a group having high interest in mechanical areas, the score takes on more meaning.

CRITERION-REFERENCED
INTERPRETATIONS

Norm-referenced interpretations of test scores have obvious limitations in instructional programming for the individual student. A student's status or position in the group may tell us little about what skills and content the student has actually mastered. We are usually interested in how well the student is meeting the instructional objectives. Attainment of instructional objectives to some criterion, such as mastery or partial mastery, takes precedence over positioning in the group of students. A student could position high on a test, and still not have met the objectives set for that student. Conversely, a student could position low on a test and have met the objectives, provided the criterion did not call for a higher level of attainment.

When an individual's performance score is interpreted with reference to an established criterion and without reference to the level of the performance of a group, we have a criterion-referenced interpretation. The criterion is usually established prior to any actual measurement being done. The criterion or criteria are usually stated in the instructional objectives or in supplements to the stated objectives. For example, a list of objectives may have an accompanying statement indicating that when students score 90 percent correct on the related test, they should be considered as having attained the objectives. The criterion for a specific test may be derived in various ways. The following two sections take the reader through an example of the use and interpretation of a criterion-referenced test.

Criterion-referenced Tests and Instructional Objectives

Instructional programming for the individual student places heavy emphasis on the use of objectives and, specifically, instructional objectives set for each child (see Figure 1.1). It is not a purpose of this text to dwell on the preparation of instructional objectives (see Nussel, *et al.* 1976, Chapter 4). However, without adequate instructional objectives it is impossible to effectively conduct measurement and evaluation; there is no referent on which to base a criterion-referenced interpretation.

Many published, curriculum programs provide sets of instructional objectives. The teacher's responsibility then becomes one of selecting appropriate objectives rather than preparing them. In some cases it may be desirable to prepare supplementary objectives. In any event, a knowledge of how to prepare objectives is helpful in knowing how to select objectives.

Consider the following three example objectives that deal with the skill of structural analysis in reading (Otto and Chester 1976).

O_1: The child identifies simple contractions (e.g., I'm, it's, can't) and uses them correctly in sentences.

O_2: The child identifies the root word in familiar inflected words (e.g., jumping, catches, runs).

O_3: The child identifies the possessive forms of nouns used in context.

These objectives clearly specify the learner (child) behavior. Also, the criterion for meeting each objective implies mastery.*

Assessment exercises are then prepared to measure the attainment of these three objectives. A teacher-devised item or exercise relative to O_2 might be to give individual children a list of inflected words, have each one read each word, and identify the root word. The exercises might be collected into a test, either written or oral, and the test administered.

Suppose that before the test is administered to any student an 80 percent correct criterion is established as the minimum performance required for mastery of each objective. A student who does not attain the criterion has not mastered the skill sufficiently to move ahead in the instructional sequence. The criterion is to a large extent

---

* A supplementary statement indicates that that child should score 80 percent or more correct on a related test as evidence of having attained any particular objective. Schools are advised to modify as appropriate the 80 percent criterion, based on their actual experiences with it.

based on teacher judgment. No magic, universal criterion for mastery exists although some curriculum materials which contain criterion-referenced tests do suggest criteria for mastery. Also, unless objectives are appropriate and the criterion for achievement relevant, there is little meaning in the attainment of a criterion regardless of what it is.

It is important to note that the criterion applies to the exercises of each objective, not to the entire test collectively. For these particular objectives it is necessary to differentiate between the different skills that the objectives represent.

In order to illustrate the criterion with the suggested exercise for O_2, if the list of inflected words contained 15 words, the student would be required to respond correctly on 12 or more words in order to be judged as having attained mastery of the objective. Note that the criterion now becomes explicit in the context of the specific exercise.

Interpreting Scores of Criterion-referenced Tests

The most parsimonious interpretation of a score on a criterion-referenced test is simply that the objectives reflected by the test either have or have not been met to whatever criteria have been established. In the example above, either O_2 is met or not met since the criterion established was mastery. Similar decisions could be made for O_1 and O_3. At least this is the beginning point for the interpretation.

Suppose that the student meets the criterion of 80 percent for each objective (Step 6 of the IPM). Clearly the objectives have been attained and the student is ready to implement the next sequence in the program or take other appropriate actions (Step 7 of the IPM). If the objectives had not been attained, the criterion had not been reached, an analysis would be made of where the student's performance was deficient. Possibly only one objective, say O_3, was not attained. Whatever the pattern of nonmastery, reassessment of the student's characteristics, the learning mode, etc., would be made and appropriate action taken (Step 7 of the IPM).

Note that throughout the administration of the test and the interpretation of the student's performance, no reference is made to other students in the school or to some other reference group outside the school. All interpretation is based on the criterion. Student performance is important only as it relates to the criterion. That characteristic makes for criterion-referenced assessment.

The example discussed above is concentrated in Steps 6 and 7 of the IPM. These are not the only points in an instructional sequence where assessment takes place or assessment results are interpreted. Each student's status is also assessed before actual instruction begins

(Step 3 of the IPM). Assessment in objective-based instruction is criterion-referenced because the results of the tests are compared with criteria of specific objectives rather than to the performance of a normative group dealing with unspecified objectives.

EVALUATION AND INSTRUCTION

The evaluation and measurement of major concern to all teachers and children are those dealing with instruction. In IGE, each teacher is not solely responsible for the entire task nor is evaluation conducted in isolation by individual teachers, but cooperatively by the unit staff. Unit leaders assume leadership for planning evaluation activities but every teacher has a responsibility to contribute to the effort.

In Figure 1.1, it was noted that evaluation is a continuing activity throughout any instructional sequence. Thus, evaluation is basically a continuous function of the instructional process. To some extent this has been true of traditional instruction in the elementary school, but testing and evaluation were identified more as culminating activities. Midterm, six weeks, etc., exams were given with norm-referenced interpretations of the results primarily for the purpose of designating grades. Evaluation often became an activity adjunct to the instruction. This is not the case in IGE. Evaluation is a part of instruction and a very important part.

Evaluation in instructional programming for the individual student focuses upon the two kinds of decisions required of the staff in an IGE school. These decisions were introduced earlier in the chapter and they are mentioned here as a reminder for the reader. Decisions about the performance of individual students are basically student evaluation; each student's performance is evaluated individually with respect to the objectives set for that student. The second kind of decision relates to the effectiveness of instructional programs, and this requires the evaluation of programs (or components of programs). Of course, the performance of students is involved in the evaluation of programs, but the focus is not on each individual's performance. Chapter 7 presents a detailed description of evaluating instructional programs.

Basic Questions of Instructional Evaluation

Regardless of whether evaluation is focused toward how well individual students learn and attain their objectives or the instructional programs of the students, there are general questions applicable to evaluation. The evaluation of student learning and the evaluation of instructional programs differ primarily in their purpose. To some

The student is a primary source of information used for evaluation purposes.

extent, the form and use of results differ but the general questions still apply.

As a part of every instructional sequence, evaluation focuses primarily on securing answers to the following questions:*

---

* These questions are compatible with and to a large extent synonymous with the model for analyzing decision making presented in Chapter 1 of J. Lipham and M. Fruth 1976. *The Principal and Individually Guided Education*. Reading, Mass.: Addison-Wesley.

1. What are the decision points in the instructional process?
2. What are the sources of information?
3. What information is required for decision making?
4. How is the information obtained?
5. When is the information obtained?
6. How is the information summarized and reported?
7. How is the information used at the decision points?

Answering these questions involves the kinds of activities discussed earlier in the chapter. The evaluation system can be related more specifically to the IPM and illustrated using the reading example discussed earlier. Three objectives were used in that example (p. 15) and the criterion of acceptable performance was set at 80 percent correct on the appropriate exercises for each objective. The evaluation system follows the sequence described below. (The numbers in the sequence correspond with the numbers of the questions.)

1. O_1, O_2, and O_3 are identified and the decision point will be at the close of the instruction related to these three objectives; alternatives at the decision point are (1) the student has mastery or (2) the student does not have mastery and an appropriate course of action is followed depending upon the extent and type of deficiency.

   The objectives are formulated at Step 3 and at Step 4 of the IPM. However, the decision point is identified at the conclusion of Step 6 with Step 7 being the alternative.

2. The source of information is the individual student.

3. Information required consists of performance on the exercises (either oral or written) that reflect mastery of the objectives. For example one part of the information is the student score on the 15-word list of inflected words.

4. The information is obtained by "testing" the student—giving the student the opportunity to perform the required skill.

5. The information is obtained after the student has presumably received adequate instruction, as judged by one or more teachers.

6. The information to be summarized consists of the performance scores relative to the three objectives. Note that the way the criteria are specified, performance for each objective must be summarized individually. If performance does not meet the criterion, information on the extent of deficiency would also be required.

7. At Step 7 the information is used (this is the decision point). If the criterion is attained the next sequence in the program is implemented; if the criterion is not attained appropriate action is taken. For example, suppose that a student misses 14 of the 15 inflected words. Reassessment of necessary prerequisite skills is in order and it is likely the skill must be entirely retaught. If 11 of 15 words had been done correctly, possibly limited supplementary instruction is all that is required before the student can proceed to the next sequence in the program.

The majority of evaluation activities of the example above takes place within Steps 6 and 7 of the IPM. The evaluation activities are sequential but at any given time the teachers of a unit will have evaluation related to several objectives in process concurrently. A given student may be at one point with reading objectives, and at another point with mathematics objectives, for example. Small groups of individual objectives may be evaluated on a short-term basis, then a larger composite of objectives evaluated which covers a longer instructional period. The extent of information used and the alternatives of the decision points will depend upon the objectives being evaluated.

The example above illustrates a short-term, summative, evaluation of individual student learning. If the information were used for making adjustments in instruction, formative evaluation would be involved. Thus, the type of evaluation depends upon the purpose for which information is being used.

EVALUATION AT VARIOUS LEVELS WITHIN THE SCHOOL BUILDING

In IGE evaluation occurs at three levels (1) each individual student, (2) particular groups of students instructed by certain teachers, and (3) all the students enrolled in the school. The corresponding students and adults involved are for (1) a student and a particular teacher, for (2) the students and their teachers that form each I & R Unit, and for (3) the students of the school and the IIC of the school building. We have already seen how evaluation at the first two levels may proceed.

Evaluation Concerns of the IIC

The group responsible for the school-level evaluation is the IIC. The IIC comprises the unit leaders and the principal, with the principal being the chairperson of the IIC. Thus, as the unit leader assumes leadership responsibility within the unit staff, the principal does so within the IIC.

There are two categories of evaluation activities at the school level that are the concern of the IIC. One is the coordination of evaluation activities of the school that relate to the students, and the other is the evaluation of the instructional and administrative staff with respect to how effectively they perform.

In the first step of the IPM the educational objectives of the student population of the building are established. This is a task of the IIC and it cannot be accomplished in an informational void. Therefore, some evaluation must take place in order to initiate this task. This evaluation relates directly to the students of the school.

As curriculum development takes place in an IGE school, this too must be evaluated by the IIC. Related instructional materials and methods must also be evaluated. The management of resources within the school is the concern of the IIC. This function invariably involves evaluation in order to eliminate deficiencies in the resource management.

An IGE school should have a defined, organized, and active program of home-school-community relations. Such a program involves numerous components such as an efficient communications system. In order to keep the program of home-school-community relations operational, systematic evaluation of the program is necessary. Again, this is a responsibility of the IIC.

Just as a unit is part of the organization of the building, a single building is usually one of several in a school system. Most school systems have some type of evaluation that originates from the central office. An example might be the administration of a standardized achievement test at a given point in the school year. (These are usually norm-referenced tests.) The schools participate in such evaluations and it is the IIC's responsibility to direct the necessary activities in a given school.

Almost all schools, especially IGE schools, have programs of staff development or inservice. These programs should be evaluated not only on how effectively they are operated, but also on their effects upon the school staff. Formal or informal evaluation of individual teachers, unit leaders, aides, etc., is also a necessary activity. In an IGE school it is the responsibility of the IIC to ensure that these kinds of staff evaluations are conducted.

The evaluation concerns of the IIC are related to providing the best instructional programs for individual students in the school. They may not appear as directly related as the evaluation that takes place within the unit but, nevertheless, this is their ultimate intent. The functions for which evaluation responsibilities lie with the IIC can be listed as follows:

1. Coordination of instruction, policy, and operation within the school.

2. Staff development and evaluation.

3. Curriculum development.

4. Resource management at the school level.

5. Establishing educational objectives.

6. Home-school-community relations.

7. School systemwide assessment.

In the multiunit school organization there are complete channels for communication, both input and feedback, among the unit, the building level, and the system level. The unit leader is the unit's liaison to the IIC. At the system level, the organization that parallels the IIC is the systemwide program committee (SPC). Representation on the SPC may vary among school systems depending upon unique system characteristics such as the number of IGE schools. In any case, the school does have representation on the SPC through the building principal, unit leader, or teacher representatives. Evaluation input and feedback should go through these representatives.

SUMMARY

This chapter has provided an introduction to the terms measurement and evaluation as they apply to instructional programming for individual students. Assessment, measurement, and evaluation activities were identified and described. It is important that evaluation be viewed as an integral part of individualized instruction, not some kind of adjunct activity that takes place occasionally. Indeed, without assessment and evaluation instructional programming for the individual student would break down.

The difference between norm-referenced and criterion-referenced interpretations of data was described. The distinguishing characteristic between norm-referenced and criterion-referenced assessment is the interpretation of the data, not the form of item construction, length of test, or other technical features. Examples of norm-referenced and criterion-referenced assessment were provided.

It is important that the reader realize that there are two major foci of evaluation when individualizing instruction. These foci are the performance of individual students and the instructional programs. We talk about different types of evaluation such as formative and summative or process and product. These are descriptors that are helpful in orienting the purposes of evaluation activities, but in themselves do not define specific evaluation activities.

Most of the assessment when programming instruction for the individual student is criterion-referenced, and it, of necessity, is objective-based. Norm-referenced assessment is occasionally necessary and some examples were provided in the chapter. Misuses of norm-referenced testing were discussed. Although misuses are less likely to occur in an IGE school than in a traditional, age-graded school, caution should still be exercised against such misuses.

Finally, there was a brief discussion of evaluation at various levels within the school building. One of the strengths of the multiunit school is its organization, not only at the unit level but also at the school and system levels. The organization has been presented in detail in other texts (see, for example, Nussel, et al. 1976). The important point for evaluation is that the teacher be aware of evaluation at levels other than the unit. The teacher can participate in the evaluation activities as appropriate and has the opportunity for input through the organizational channels.

DISCUSSION TOPICS

1. Many times in educational situations the administration of tests and the accumulation of data on student performance have been called evaluation. Why are these activities in themselves not adequate to be considered evaluation?

2. Give two reasons why designating the average performance of a normative group as a criterion is highly inappropriate when programming instruction for the individual student.

3. Discuss the types of decision points that are most commonly included for instruction.

4. Suppose that a set of five test questions is presented to a teacher. Why is it impossible to determine from the questions themselves whether they are part of a norm-referenced or criterion-referenced test? Discuss what does distinguish between these two types of tests.

REFERENCES

H. J. Klausmeier, et al. in press. IGE, concepts and principles, Madison, Wisc.: Wisconsin Research and Development Center for Cognitive Learning.

————, and W. Goodwin 1975. Learning and human abilities, 4th ed., Harper & Row, New York, Chapter 18.

Lipham, J. M., *et al.* 1976. *The principal and individually guided education.* Reading, Mass.: Addison-Wesley.

Nussel, E., J. Inglis, and W. Wiersma 1976. *The teacher and individually guided education.* Reading, Mass.: Addison-Wesley.

Otto, W. R., and R. D. Chester 1976. *Objective-based reading.* Reading, Mass.: Addison-Wesley.

Scriven, M., "The methodology of evaluation. In R. Tyler *et al.* (eds.), *Perspectives of Curriculum Evaluation.* AERA Monograph Series on Curriculum Evaluation, No. 3, Chicago, Rand McNally, pp. 39–83.

Stufflebeam, D. L., *et al.* 1971. *Educational evaluation and decision making.* Phi Delta Kappa, Bloomington, Indiana.

2
Basic Measurement Concepts

Objectives

After reading this chapter, the reader will be able:

- To explain test validity and evaluate the validity of tests.
- To explain test reliability and interpret test scores with regard to their accuracy.
- To compute and interpret basic descriptive statistics for a set of test scores.
- To compute and interpret common item analysis indexes for norm-referenced or criterion-referenced tests.

This chapter provides an understanding of several basic measurement concepts. Some of the statistical terms are best illustrated through computational examples, but the emphasis of the chapter is on the interpretation of the statistics rather than on the computation. We will stress how teachers can use criterion-referenced tests in the classroom. The goal will be that of ensuring that teachers can judge whether the tests that they use are reliable and valid for their purposes. To do so, we must be sure that teachers* understand what it means, psychometrically, to have reliable and valid tests.

This chapter is also the appropriate place for a brief discussion of the statistics used in norm-referenced tests. Some readiness and scholastic aptitude tests that teachers will encounter when programming instruction for the individual student are norm-referenced tests. Some treatment of these statistics is necessary so that such scores are accurately interpreted.

SCALES OF MEASUREMENT

Measures of student instructional outcomes are rarely as precise as those of physical characteristics such as height and weight. The attributes measured are more difficult to define and the units of measure are usually not physical units. The result is that the scales vary in their sophistication. Terms which describe the kinds of precision inherent in the scales are; nominal, ordinal, interval, and ratio.

Nominal Measurement

The least sophisticated scales are those which merely classify objects or events by assigning numbers to them. These numbers are arbitrary and imply no quantification. For example, one could nominally measure religion by assigning Catholics the numeral 1, Protestants 2, Jews 3, and Muslims 4. These assignments are arbitrary and no arithmetic would be meaningful. One plus two does not equal three because a Catholic plus a Protestant does not equal a Jew.

Ordinal Measurement

Ordinal scales classify but they also assign rank order. An example of ordinal measurement would be rank in class on a test. Students could be ordered from first, second, third, and so forth. Such a scale gives more information than nominal measurement but it still has limitations. The units of ordinal measurement are most likely unequal. The number of points separating the first and second students probably

---

*   The term, teachers, as used includes prospective teachers, certified teachers, unit leaders, and principals.

does not equal the number separating the fifth and sixth students. These unequal units of measurement are analogous to a ruler in which some "inches" are longer than others. Addition and subtraction of such units yield meaningless numbers.

Interval Measurement

In order to be able to add and subtract scores we go to interval measurement, sometimes called equal interval measurement. This measurement scale contains the nominal and ordinal properties but is also characterized by equal units between score points. Examples include thermometers and calendar years. The difference between 10° and 20° is the same as the difference between 47° and 57°. Likewise the difference in length of time between 1946 and 1948 equals the difference between 1973 and 1975. These measures are defined in terms of physical properties such that these intervals are equal, for example, a year is the time it takes for the earth to orbit the sun. The advantage of equal units of measurement should be obvious. Sums and differences now make sense both numerically and logically. Note, however, that the zero point in interval measurement is really an arbitrary decision, for example, 0° does not mean that there is no temperature.

Ratio Measurement

The most sophisticated type of measurement includes all the preceding properties except that the zero point is nonarbitrary. In this case a score of zero indicates the absence of the quantity being measured. For example, if a man's wealth equalled zero he would have no wealth at all. This is unlike a social studies test where missing every item, that is receiving a score of zero may not indicate the complete absence of social studies knowledge. Ratio measurement is rarely achieved in educational assessment either in cognitive or affective areas. The desirability of having ratio measurement scales is that it would allow ratio comparisons such as Ann is 1½ times as tall as her little sister Mary. We can seldom say that one's intelligence or achievement is 1½ times as great as that of another person. An IQ of 120 may be 1½ times as great numerically as an IQ of 80, but a person with an IQ of 120 is not 1½ times as intelligent as a person with an IQ of 80.

Most educational measurements are better than strictly nominal or ordinal measures but few can meet the rigorous requirements of interval measurement. Educational testing is usually somewhere between ordinal and interval scales. Fortunately, empirical studies have shown that arithmetic operations on these scales are appropriate and strong bases for decision making can be obtained from even these measures.

It is important to note that carefully designed tests over a specified domain of possible items, as might be indicated in an objective, can approach ratio measurement. For example, an objective might concern miltiplication facts for pairs of numbers less than 10 that might appear on the test. However, the teacher might randomly select five or ten test problems to give to a particular student. Then, the proportion of items that the student gets correct could be used to estimate how many of the fifty possible items the student has mastered. If the student answers four of five items correctly, it is legitimate to estimate that the student would get 40 of the 50 items correct if all 50 of the items were administered. This is possible because the set of possible items was specifically defined in the objective and the test items were a random, representative sample from that set.

At times ratio interpretation can also be achieved. Say that Mary gets four of five items correct and Ann gets two of five items correct. It follows then, that if both tests were random samples from the fifty possible items, we can estimate that Mary has mastered twice as many multiplication facts as Ann.

If we twist this example to a criterion-referenced situation, a similar use can be shown. Suppose that the mastery level for the multiplication facts was set at 100 percent. That is, students would be expected to answer all items correctly, when given a ten-item test where items are randomly selected from the fifty multiplication facts. If Bill gets five of the ten items correct, it is correct to say that he is halfway there in terms of mastering the multiplication facts. Ratio statements could be made relative to another person or to the criterion of the objective as long as the set of possible items is specified and the test items are a representative sample drawn from that set. Readers interested in pursuing these points should see Harris's (1974) recent article.

DESCRIPTIVE STATISTICS

The term "statistics" often brings abhorrent visual images to some classroom teachers. Some believe that only a mathematical genius could cope with such abstractions. Although we disagree strongly, critics are correct that teachers of statistics frequently try to cover more than classroom teachers really need to know. We will, therefore, resist temptation and limit our scope to what the teacher needs to know to interpret test scores, and to understand the technical meaning of reliability and validity.

Statistics are merely numbers which synthesize large quantities of scores. It is frequently more efficient to report a single value than it is to report the score of every individual. For example, suppose that a teacher gave a 30-item test over one instructional objective to 40 students. It would not be reasonable to cite the score for each student whenever the test scores are referred to. Instead a summary value which in some way describes the distribution of scores would be more useful. There are different measures that can be used to describe distributions.

Say, for example, that an objective on punctuation called for the students to recognize 45 of 50 punctuation errors in an essay. The scores for a group of twenty-five students appears in Table 2.1. It is easier to analyze the distribution of scores if the scores are arranged in a frequency distribution. Table 2.2 indicates the frequency distribution for the same set of scores. First, scores in the frequency distribution are listed in rank order from the highest to the lowest. Then a second column indicates the frequency, or number of persons who received each score. For example, three students received 47, two received 40, and so forth.

It is easy now to see that 13 of the 25 students were above the criterion on this test. That is, 0.52 of the class have mastered the objective. The teacher would probably also note that another seven students, or 0.28 of the class, came within five points of mastering the objective. The remaining five students, the lowest 20 percent of the class, were even further below the criterion. Decisions about individual students would surely be based on the kinds of errors that were

Table 2.1 Scores of 25 Students on a 50-item Test

Student	Score	Student	Score
A	48	N	43
B	50	O	47
C	46	P	48
D	41	Q	42
E	37	R	44
F	48	S	38
G	38	T	49
H	47	U	34
I	49	V	35
J	44	W	47
K	48	X	40
L	49	Y	48
M	40		

Table 2.2 Frequency Distribution of 25 Scores

Score	Frequency	Cumulative Frequency
50	1	25
49	3	24
48	5	21
47	3	16
46	1	13
45	0	12
44	2	12
43	1	10
42	1	9
41	1	8
40	2	7
39	0	5
38	2	5
37	1	3
36	0	2
35	1	2
34	1	1

made and their nearness to the criterion. The entire distribution, though, could be summarized with other descriptive statistics.

Measures of Central Tendency: Norm-referenced Statistics

Three measures of central tendency are commonly used to describe sets of test scores. The easiest to find is the *mode*, the most frequently occurring score. The mode of the set of test scores in Table 2.1 is 48. A score of 48 appears five times, and no other score occurs as often.

The *mean* of the set of scores equals the arithmetic average of the scores which is found by summing all the scores and dividing by the number of scores. Adding the twenty-five scores together yields 1100, and 1100 divided by 25 equals 44. Hence, the mean of this set of scores equals 44.

The other measure of central tendency is the *median*. The median is the point which divides the distribution in half, that is, half of the scores fall above the median and half of the scores fall below the median. The rightmost column in Table 2.2 contains the cumulative sum of the frequencies which indicates how many persons scored at or below a particular score. For example, for this set of test scores, twenty-one persons scored at or below a raw score of 48. We can calculate the median from the column of cumulative frequencies. The middle score in the distribution is 46 since there are twelve scores above it and twelve scores below. Hence, 46 is the median. For a distribution with an even number of scores, the median would be halfway between the two middle scores. If a distribution had many ties in the middle of the distribution, one would have to interpolate to get the exact median. Such precision is not needed for most classroom tests, so the whole number closest to the middle of the distribution will usually suffice.

Each of these three measures of central tendency, the mean, median, and mode, is a legitimate definition of average performance on this test. When the principal asks, "How did the students score on your test?", the teacher can now respond accurately and concisely. The principal will know that half of the class scored below 46 and that more persons received 48 than any other score and that the arithmetic average was 44.

Measures of Dispersion: Norm-referenced Statistics

The teacher is usually interested in more than the central tendency of a set of test scores. Teachers might also wonder whether the students tended to differ widely on the test or whether their scores were grouped closely about the mean. Two of the commonly used descriptive statistics which quantify the dispersion, or spread among the scores, are the range and the standard deviation. Each of these indicates how widely separated the scores tend to be, but they consider different information.

Range. The range indicates the difference between the highest and lowest scores in the distribution of scores. There are actually two ranges, the inclusive range and the exclusive range. This should never be confusing though because a reported range should be clearly designated as either an inclusive or exclusive range.

The inclusive range is the difference between the upper real limit of the highest score in the distribution and the lower real limit of the lowest score in the distribution. For the data reported in Table 2.1, the highest score is 50 and thus the highest real limit is 50.5 while the lowest score is 34 so the lowest real limit is 33.5. The difference between these real limits (50.5 − 33.5) equals 17. The inclusive range for the distribution in Table 2.1 is 17.

The exclusive range is merely the difference between the highest score and the lowest score in the distribution, e.g., 50 − 34 = 16. The exclusive range *excludes* the real limits but it is slightly easier to calculate. Note that when the test score is the number of items answered correctly, the inclusive range equals the exclusive range plus one. Classroom teachers would more likely use the exclusive range because of its simplicity.

A problem with using either of these ranges is that only the two most extreme scores are used in the computation. There is no indication of the spread of scores between the highest and lowest. A measure of dispersion which takes into consideration every score in the distribution is the standard deviation. The standard deviation is used a great deal in interpreting scores from standardized achievement or aptitude tests.

Standard Deviation. In words, the standard deviation is the square root of the average squared deviation from the mean. As a formula, it looks like this:

$$\text{Standard Deviation} = \sqrt{\frac{\Sigma\,(\text{Score} - \text{Mean})^2}{N}}$$

where Σ, capital sigma, is the summation operator and N is the number of scores in the distribution. The computation of the standard deviation for the data in Table 2.1 is illustrated in Table 2.3. The data for students K through V are omitted to save space but these values are included in the column totals.

The standard deviation is a distance in raw score points that in-

Table 2.3 Computation of the Standard Deviation

Student	Score	Score − Mean	(Score − Mean)²
A	48	4	16
B	50	6	36
C	46	2	4
D	41	−3	9
E	37	−7	49
F	48	4	16
G	38	−6	36
H	47	3	9
I	49	5	25
J	44	0	0
.	.	.	.
.	.	.	.
.	.	.	.
W	47	3	9
X	40	−4	16
Y	48	4	16
	1100	0	570

$$\text{S.D.} = \sqrt{\frac{570}{25}} = \sqrt{22.8} = 4.77.$$

dicates how widely spread about the mean are the scores in the distribution. The usefulness of the standard deviation becomes apparent when scores from different tests are compared.

Suppose that a test of fractions and a reading comprehension test were given to the same class. The fractions test had a mean of 30 and a standard deviation of 8. The reading comprehension test had a mean of 60 and a standard deviation of 10. If John scored 38 on the fractions test and 55 on the reading comprehension test, it would appear from the raw scores that he did better in reading than in fractions because 55 is greater than 38. But, relative to the performance of the others in the class, the exact opposite is true. A score of 38 on the fractions test is one standard deviation above the mean, a score that is much better than average. A score of 55 on the reading comprehension test is one-half of a standard deviation below the mean, a score that is lower than average. Clearly, when comparison is made relative to the class mean, John's performance on the fractions test is better than his performance on the reading comprehension test. Note that this is a norm-referenced example as John is being compared to the group mean rather than to a criterion.

Sometimes the dispersion of test scores is indicated by a statistic called the *variance*. The variance is merely the standard deviation squared. It provides much the same information as the standard deviation but is more tractable in developing much of the theory of measurement.

In criterion-referenced testing, the measures of central tendency and dispersion are useful, but not of primary concern. Criterion-referenced scores are interpreted relative to an established criterion rather than relative to the mean. It is more useful to speak of the *proportion* of the class which scores above a criterion than it is to speak of average performance on a criterion-referenced test.

Correlation

One other statistic is commonly used in measurement. That statistic is the correlation coefficient which quantifies the direction and degree of relationship between two variables. There sometimes is some confusion about the term correlation because it often has many different meanings for different people. In statistical terms the correlation between two variables is a precise value that quantifies the association between the two variables. Correlation is expressed as a numerical coefficient.

The correlation coefficient is a number which can range between -1 and $+1$. A graph, or scatterplot, of the pairs of scores for two variables can be plotted to give a visual illustration of the relationship between the two variables.

For example, suppose that eight students each take two tests, one in reading and one in science. Each test comprises ten items. The pairs of scores and the scatterplot appear in Figure 2.1. Notice that persons with low scores in reading also tend to have low scores in science. Similarly, persons with high scores in reading tend to have high scores in science. Such a direct relationship has a *positive* direction. Inverse relations are said to have *negative* direction.

Student	Reading	Science
Bill	4	7
Ann	3	2
Paul	7	6
Jim	8	8
Pete	3	5
Mary	5	8
Jane	10	7
Sue	2	4

Fig. 2.1 Scatterplot of reading and science scores.

The formula for calculating the Pearson product-moment correlation coefficient is:

$$r = \frac{N\Sigma XY - \Sigma X\Sigma Y}{\sqrt{[N\Sigma X^2 - (\Sigma X)^2][N\Sigma Y^2 - (\Sigma Y)^2]}}.$$

The necessary data from Figure 2.1 appear below:

X	Y	X^2	Y^2	XY
4	7	16	49	28
3	2	9	4	6
7	6	49	36	42
8	8	64	64	64
3	5	9	25	15
5	8	25	64	40
10	7	100	49	70
3	5	9	25	15
43	48	281	316	280

This works out to

$$r = \frac{8 \times 280 - 43 \times 48}{\sqrt{(8 \times 281 - 43^2)\ (8 \times 316 - 48^2)}} = 0.58.$$

A correlation of +0.58 indicates a moderate degree of association between the two variables. The points of the scatterplot could be contained by an ellipse indicating some departure from the straight line, characteristic of perfect correlation.

Other degrees of association are illustrated by the scatterplots in Figure 2.2. As you can see, the direction of the relationship is indi-

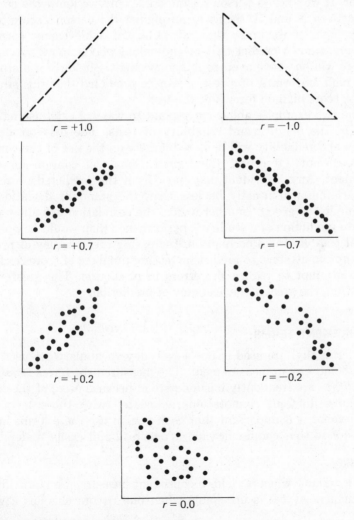

Fig. 2.2 Scatterplots for various correlations.

cated by the sign and the strength of the relationship is indicated by the closeness to +1 or −1. Correlations close to zero indicate no relationship between the variables.

Correlation is useful in measurement because it can be used to quantify how well one can predict, or correlate (1) scores on a test with scores on some external measure of performance, or (2) performances on a parallel test covering the same objectives. In fact, the psychometric definitions of the terms *reliability* and *validity*, as we shall see later in this chapter, are based largely on correlational statements.

Correlations are used to make predictions from one variable to another. If we know a person's score on X, and we know the correlation between X and Y, then we can predict the person's score on Y. For example, if we know that aptitude and achievement correlate positively, we can predict that an individual who is above average in aptitude will be above average in achievement. Similarly if a student scores high on form A of a test, it can be predicted that this student will also score high on form B of the test.

The two examples above correspond to ways of establishing estimates of the validity and reliability of tests. The development of validity and reliability will be based largely on the use of the correlation coefficient. Of course these predictions will contain an error component. Any individual may vary from the predicted score but this variation will usually be less than the standard deviation for everyone in the group. In other words, the correlation will allow more accurate prediction of a student's performance than would be possible without establishing a correlation. Increasing the accuracy of prediction is *not* an attempt to predict increasing numbers of scores exactly, but an attempt to reduce the errors in prediction. The greater the correlation, the greater the accuracy of prediction.

MEASUREMENT TERMS

Some terms that are used in one's everyday vocabulary are used in a very specific way in measurement. The measurement terms *reliability* and *validity* are frequently misunderstood because users of the terms often have different connotations associated with those terms. In measurement it is important that each person use these terms in the same way so that communication is accurate and easily understood.

Reliability

A test is reliable when it yields a consistent measure of an individual's performance. A test is unreliable when one's score changes a great deal from one administration of the test to another. For example, a test would be considered unreliable if the person who scored highest in a class of 30 one time scored only at the median of the class when the test was given again two days later. Similarly if a student took two forms of a test for a particular objective and was above criterion on one form and below criterion on the other form, one would question the reliability of the forms.

There are several ways to develop the concept of reliability. The reader who is interested in pursuing this topic in greater depth is referred to the suggested references at the end of this chapter. For our purposes, the following development should be enough to allow teachers to correctly use the terms.

Consider the reliability of a test for a particular objective which requires the student to tell the time when the clock hands are set at the minute marks. A test is constructed to measure whether the student can tell time as specified in the objective. There are 720 possible clock positions that could be included in the test. It is more likely that only five or ten items will be used on the test. If five items are randomly selected from the total number of possible items, then the performance of a student on those items is a representative estimate of how this student would do if given all of the possible items.

If a student would take all of the possible items for a particular objective, the score would be this student's *true score;* the observed test score is only an estimate of the true score. The difference between the observed score and the true score is *error.*

$$X = T + e$$

The true score is unknown and unobservable. Fortunately the observed score is known and the error component can be estimated. Therefore, the true score can be estimated.

The mathematics of reliability theory will not be presented here but some attention must be given to the conceptual development. The correlation of the five-item time-telling test with the domain of all possible tests equals the square root of the reliability coefficient. The reliability coefficient is the average correlation of one test with all the tests in the domain. In other words, the square root of the reliability coefficient equals the correlation of the observed test score with the unobservable true score.

$$r_{1T} = r_{11}$$

where r_{1T} is the correlation of the test (1) with the true score (T) and r_{11} is the reliability coefficient. Methods of estimating the reliability coefficient are presented below.

The reliability coefficient is a number ranging from 0 to 1, which indicates the proportion of variance in the raw scores that is due to students differing in their true scores. The difference between the reliability coefficient and unity equals the proportion of the variance in raw scores that is due to measurement error. Think of a test with a reliability coefficient of 0.80. The bulk, in this case 80 percent, of the difference in raw scores is due to differences in true scores. Measurement error accounts for only 20 percent of the raw score variance.

Estimating the reliability of a test. To estimate the reliability of a test, one must get empirical evidence of the consistency or stability of performance of individuals across sets of items from a specified domain or across time. The usual methods are: (1) to correlate performance over two testings to determine whether scores remain relatively stable, or (2) to use a formula which estimates how well one would do on all of the items in a domain, based on one's performance on a set of representative items. Numerous ways of gathering such data exist; we shall present four of the most frequently used methods.

Test-retest reliability. The simplest method for gathering the data necessary for estimating the reliability of a test is merely to give the same test to the same group of people on two separate occasions. The pairs of scores for each person constitute X and Y values for the correlation formula given earlier. The correlation coefficient that is computed then becomes the reliability coefficient.

Alternate forms reliability. A problem with test-retest reliability is that the same test items are given each time. Since the items on a particular test constitute such a small proportion of the items in the domain of possible items, it makes little sense to use only that small subset in establishing the reliability of that test for a particular sample of students. The natural consequence is then to construct two parallel tests and administer both of them to the same group of people. The pairs of scores can then be correlated and, again, that correlation is the reliability coefficient for the tests.

The advantage of the alternate forms technique (also called parallel forms) is that the domain of content is better sampled. A more practical advantage is that students taking two different forms of a test will cooperate better than students who are given exactly the same test on two occasions. The disadvantage of the alternate forms technique is that two tests must be constructed. This is a major problem because the tests must be parallel in content, format, difficulty, and statistical properties. Both the alternate forms and test-retest methods require two test administrations. The following two methods of estimating test reliability overcome that practical problem.

Split-half reliability. The split-half procedure essentially performs an alternate forms reliability estimate within one test. The test is so constructed that the items can be separated into two parallel parts. The scores of each student on the two halves of the tests are then correlated. That computation yields a reliability coefficient for a test half as long as the full test. The reliability of the test of full length can then be estimated with the Spearman-Brown formula:

$$r_f = \frac{2r_{11}}{1 + r_{11}}.$$

where r_f is the estimate of reliability for the test of full length and r_{11} is the correlation between the two halves of the test.

Note that each of these three methods of estimating the reliability of a test require data that indicate the stability or consistency of test performance across time or across sets of items. Figure 2.3 illustrates the scatterplots that are involved in each of these reliability coefficients. One other commonly used method of finding a reliability coefficient does not require the calculation of a correlation coefficient. This technique was developed by Kuder and Richardson (1937).

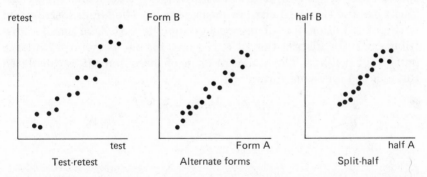

Fig. 2.3 Scatterplots of data used in computing reliability coefficients through correlation.

Kuder-Richardson formulas. The Kuder and Richardson formulas are not based on the correlation of two tests or two halves of tests. Rather, the average correlation among the items on the test is found and then the general Spearman-Brown formula is used to raise this value to correspond to a test of full length. The result is a reliability coefficient that measures the internal consistency of performance across the items on the test. The most frequently used Kuder-Richardson formula is the KR_{20} which requires that items are scored as right or wrong.

$$r_{\mathrm{KR}_{20}} = \frac{K}{K-1}\left[1 - \frac{\Sigma pq}{\sigma^2}\right]$$

where K = the number of items on the test
p = the proportion of persons getting an item correct
$q = 1 - p$
σ^2 = the variance of total test scores

To calculate the KR_{20}, it is necessary to find the proportion of persons who get each item correct, the proportion who get each item incorrect, and the variance (standard deviation squared) of the total test scores. When combined in the formula above, the reliability coefficient is easily determined.

The standard error of measurement. A useful concept in reliability is the standard error of measurement. Determining the reliability of a test allows one to interpret a student's score in light of the test's accuracy. The standard error of measurement can be thought of as the standard deviation of an individual's distribution of test scores over a large number of test administrations. In other words, it gives an estimate of how stable an individual's observed test score can be expected to be as we estimate that individual's true score. Figure 2.4 illustrates the standard error of measurement. The larger distribution is the distribution for all persons taking the test. The smaller distribution is the distribution of test scores for one person over a large number of testings. The standard error of measurement is calculated through the following formula:

$$S.E.M. = \sigma\sqrt{1 - r_{11}}.$$

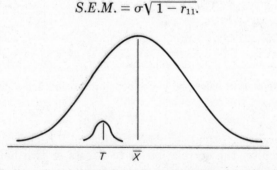

Fig. 2.4 Distribution of an individual's test scores compared with the distribution of all persons.

For example, if a test has a reliability coefficient of 0.91 and a standard deviation of 10, then the standard error measurement is:

$$10\sqrt{1 - 0.91} = 3.$$

This means that although the standard deviation for all persons is 10, scores from repeated testings for an individual would not be nearly that variable. The standard deviation of the distribution of scores for an individual would be only three raw points. In other words, the observed test score for an individual is fallible. If one took the test again it is not likely that exactly the same score would be achieved. However, the standard error of measurement allows us to estimate how widely spread, or how inconsistent, these individual scores would be.

Note that with a perfectly reliable test, where the reliability coefficient equals 1.0, the standard error of measurement would be zero. In this instance there would be no measurement error, and the test would consistently measure individuals' true scores.

Although teachers may not consistently or often compute reliability coefficients it is important to understand the concept. Published tests usually have discussions in the manual about the extent of reliability and how it was established. This information has definite implications for the selection and subsequent use of tests. All other factors being equal, the more reliable test is preferred.

Improving the reliability of tests. Tests tend to be more reliable when the directions to both the test taker and the test scorer are clear and specific. Ambiguities in either of these tasks will tend to introduce inconsistencies which will lower the reliability of the test.

The reliability of a test tends to increase with increased length. The relationship between test length and test reliability has been quantified by the Spearman-Brown formula. As the test is homogeneously lengthened the reliability coefficient increases.

For criterion-referenced tests which are based upon very specific instructional objectives, it may not be necessary to have a large number of items. This is because the items which correspond to a particular objective should be very similar. In other words, the correlations among items on the test should be very high. Such redundancy among items allows for reliable testing of a particular objective.

On norm-referenced tests reliability can be improved by maximizing the standard deviation of the distribution of test scores. This can be provided for by making each item on the test of middle difficulty; that is, half the persons miss the item and half get it correct. Item difficulty is further discussed later in this chapter.

Validity

Validity is yet another term that has many common meanings but has a specific technical definition in measurement. The validity of a test refers to whether the test measures the *attribute* that it purports to measure. The validity is usually established by determining whether the test is useful in practical or theoretical applications.

Sweeping statements are often made about a test's validity or lack of it. Actually a test may be quite valid for one purpose and at the same time be quite invalid for another purpose. If it adequately serves a given purpose, then the test is valid for that purpose. Suppose that a teacher wants to determine whether some students have mastered a particular objective. A 15-item test is prepared over the domain of items for that objective. The goal is to create items that adequately represent the domain of possible items. If the items fully represent the objective, then the test is valid for the teacher's purpose. However that same test may be very inadequate as a predictor of future success or as an indicator of scholastic aptitude.

Test validity can be categorized into three basic types. Each of these types uses different methods for establishing whether a test is valid for a particular purpose. It is important for a test maker or test user to keep in mind the type of validity which corresponds to his specific purpose.

Content validity. The content validity of a test is probably the greatest concern for teachers. The concern in the example just given was for content validity. In essence, content validity is a sampling problem. If the test items adequately represent the domain of possible items, then the test has content validity. This is the overriding concern of achievement tests. When a test is not content valid, two things happen. First, the students cannot demonstrate skills which they possess but which are not tested. Second, irrelevant items are presented which the student may not get correct only because the concepts were never taught. Both of these problems are produced by tests that are not content valid and both result in a tendency to lower the student's test score.

Criterion-related validity. A second type of test validity relates performance on a test to some external criterion. Unfortunately, this is one time when we use the word criterion in a different sense from its use in criterion-referenced testing. In the context of test validity, the criterion is performance on another test or on some measurable task. A test has criterion-related validity if the test scores are adequate predictors of the performance. For example, the Scholastic Aptitude Test (SAT) is given to high school seniors for the purpose of predicting their subsequent grade point averages as college freshmen. An accurate prediction greatly aids students in assessing their chances at various colleges that they might consider attending.

A distinction that is commonly made is to speak of two kinds of criterion-related validity, predictive and concurrent validity. *Predictive validity* refers to correlating test scores with future performance on the criterion. *Concurrent validity* refers to correlating test scores with present performance on a criterion. The distinction is made only in terms of the amount of time between measurements on the predictor test and the criterion.

Construct validity. The third and most complex kind of validity is construct validity. This validity is more of a concern for tests of psychological constructs such as intelligence and creativity than it is for achievement tests. When a test constructor establishes the construct validity of a test, logical and empirical evidence about the psychological interpretation of the test scores is given. In other words, establishing the construct validity requires that the meaning of the test score be made clear, for example, what differentiates a high scorer from a low scorer on the test; what can a high scorer on the test be predicted to do?

Establishing test validity. The three types of validity are established in very different ways. Content validity is established through a logical analysis of the match between what was taught and the items on the test. Two methods can help demonstrate the content validity of a test. One way is to list all of the specific objectives tested, then the items can be matched with the objectives to see whether all objectives are adequately assessed and to see whether all test items do correspond to relevant objectives. Another method is to construct a table of specifications which classifies the items on a test according to their content and taxonomic level, that is, student outcome required on the item. This analysis allows the teacher to judge whether the test items adequately reflect the emphasis on particular topics in the classroom. An example of a table of specifications appears in the next chapter.

In objective-based instruction the content validity analysis will necessarily be per objective, since most achievement tests will be designed to assess a student's achievements related to a particular objective. The table of specifications is more appropriate for tests of larger blocks of content. More will be said about this in the following chapter.

Criterion-related validity is established by correlating the scores of the test used for prediction with scores on the external criterion. If the correlation improves the prediction over chance, then the test possesses validity for that purpose. Standards for criterion-related validity are relative, and the size of the best predictor may vary widely depending upon the nature of the variables used as both the predictor and the criterion.

Construct validity is established through a combination of logical and empirical analyses. A test can be shown to measure what it purports to measure when:

- the test scores are positively correlated with other measures of the same construct
- the test is not correlated with tests of other constructs
- the items represent the content theoretically associated with the construct
- groups known to differ on the construct differ on the test

For example, the construct validity of a test designed to measure "intelligence" would be supported if this test was positively correlated with the Stanford-Binet Intelligence Scale, if this test was not correlated with running speed or weight, and if merit scholars did better than average on that test. Each of these bits of information adds explanatory power about what the test score really means.

Test Validity—An Example

An example of determining the validity of a published test may clarify some of the general development of test validity. Let us look closely at the Initial Consonants subtest of the *Wisconsin Tests of Reading Skill Development: I. Word Attack*. The items on this test require the student to match beginning consonant sounds of pictures. Item one (Fig. 2.5) has the student match the beginning sound of a "pen" to the beginning sound of either a crayon, a pear, or a stick.

Fig. 2.5 Item from the Initial Consonants subtest.

To establish the validity of the entire test, it is necessary to determine whether the initial consonants on the test were a representative sample of the twenty consonants that might have been selected. Such an analysis would provide information about the *content valid-*

ity of the test. The sixteen items on the subtest include fifteen of the twenty possible initial consonants. The omitted consonants appear to be those that are less frequently used. This appears to be a strength.

The inspection of every item should be a part of the validity check because teachers may find reasons for incorrect answers other than not knowing the initial consonants. For example, Item 10 calls for a match between the "f" sound from fish and fence. The picture of a "fishing rod" is considered incorrect. Similarly some pictures have words embedded in them. A "soup" can is an incorrect response, but later a "paste" jar is the correct response. In the latter case, the presence of the jar label could provide the student a clue. It is also true that six items contain incorrect choices that rhyme with the stimulus word. Since Test 1 deals with rhyming words, this is a possible point of confusion. That is, to what extent are incorrect answers a result of not following directions and looking for the wrong thing rather than the result of not knowing the content?

The *criterion-related* validity of the Initial Consonants test might be established by using these test scores as a basis for predicting teachers' ratings of readiness or performance on the related reading subtests. That is, do scores on Test 7: Initial Consonants accurately predict scores on Test 3: Shapes?

The *construct validity* of the test might in this case be appraised by seeing how the test scores fit within the "Outline of Word Attack Skills" presented by Otto and Chester (1976: Chapter 3–6). In this sequence, "initial consonants" appears above "distinguishes colors" in Level A, but below "has a basic sight vocabulary" of Level B. If we assume that the outline is correct, then the test should differentiate among students at different points in the outline. Specifically, we would expect that most children with a basic sight vocabulary could also do well on the test of initial consonants. Similarly, students who could not distinguish colors should also have difficulty with initial consonants.

In summary, establishing the validity of a test takes some time. The analysis required need not be sophisticated, but it should be thorough and systematic. When teachers select tests, they too should be thorough and systematic in requiring adequate validity information from the publishers of the tests.

ITEM ANALYSIS

Two characteristics that are frequently encountered in describing individual test items are difficulty and discrimination. These are indexes that indicate the performance of students on each item. Inspection of these indexes provides the teachers with a large amount of information about construction of items themselves and about the adequacy of their instruction.

Difficulty

Item difficulty is an index which shows the proportion of students who answered an item correctly.

$$P = \frac{\text{\# of correct responses to an item}}{\text{\# of persons responding}}.$$

For example, if an item had a difficulty level of 0.90, this would mean that 90 percent of the persons taking the test answered that item correctly. It would be a very easy item.

The difficulty index can range from 0 to 1. It is an inverse scale since high P levels correspond to easy items and low P levels correspond to difficult items. This is a possible source of confusion.

Teachers may choose to delete or revise items based on their difficulty levels. Criterion-referenced tests often are constructed from items with difficulty levels of 0.80 or 0.90. The difficulty index preferred for norm-referenced test items is about 0.50. A norm-referenced test is designed to measure individual differences and items of middle difficulty will help to spread out the scores.

An inspection of difficulty levels can be very revealing to teachers. Often there are concepts that everyone assumed were well understood but their test items have surprising difficulty levels. The teachers must then determine whether the problem lies with the test item or the instruction and what action seems necessary.

Discrimination

The other item statistic which is useful in evaluating individual items is the discrimination index, D.

$$D = \frac{\text{\# correct in top 27\% } - \text{ \# correct in bottom 27\%}}{0.27\ (N)}$$

in which N = the total number of students taking the test.

Discrimination in the norm-referenced case can be computed by

1) ordering the tests from highest score to lowest score,

2) selecting the top and bottom 27 percent of the papers (or the whole number nearest to 27 percent),

3) tallying the number of correct responses for each group on each item, and

4) combining the values as indicated in the formula above.

The discrimination index can range from -1 to $+1$. It measures how well a particular item separates the top and bottom extremes in the distribution of total test scores. Items with D values above 0.4 can be considered very effective in differentiating among levels of understanding of the concepts measured on the total test.

A negative discrimination index indicates a problem with the item. In this case those who did well on the total test tended to miss the item. Those who did poorly on the total test tended to correctly answer that same item. Clearly either the item is confusing to the better students or the instruction has resulted in some misunderstandings among the students. In either case, the teachers should investigate and take appropriate action, either deleting the item, rewriting the item, or reteaching the concept covered in the item.

In criterion-referenced tests the discrimination should be with respect to the criterion rather than among individuals. A similar discrimination index could be developed dividing students into groups depending on whether they were above or below criterion on the total test. Then the tallies of correct responses to each item would indicate how well each item separated students with respect to the criterion. When proportionally more persons who were below criterion than who were above criterion answered an item correctly, it would correspond to a negative D value.

Another discrimination measure for criterion-referenced tests could be obtained by correlating success on the item (0 or 1) with achievement relative to the test criterion (0 or 1). The correlations could be interpreted in the same way as the D index. Negative values would signal problem items and high values would indicate effective test items.

Figure 2.6 illustrates how item analysis tallies might appear for a five-item criterion-referenced test for a particular objective. Suppose that 30 students took the test and 20 (N_A) were above criterion. The

Item	$N_A = 20$ # correct Above criterion (A)	$N_B = 10$ # correct Below criterion (B)	Diffi- culty	Discrimi- nation
1	18	6	0.80	.30
2	20	0	0.66	1.00
3	10	10	0.66	-0.50
4	17	4	0.70	0.45
5	16	7	0.76	0.10

Fig. 2.6 Example of item analysis.

remaining ten students (N_B) were below criterion. Then the unit teachers or aides would tally the number of correct answers to each question for these two groups of students.

The difficulty index is then

$$\frac{A + B}{N_A + N_B}$$

and discrimination would be

$$\frac{A}{N_A} - \frac{B}{N_B}.$$

For Item 1 in Figure 2.6, the computations are:

$$A = 18 \quad \frac{A}{N_A} = \frac{18}{20} = 0.9. \qquad \frac{B}{N_B} = \frac{6}{10} = 0.6.$$
$$B = 6$$

$$\text{Difficulty} \quad = \frac{18 + 6}{20 + 10} = 0.8.$$

$$\text{Discrimination} = 0.9 - 0.6 = 0.3.$$

Note that this index would not be appropriate if either N_A or N_B were small (for example, less than five).

A quick inspection of the discrimination and difficulty indexes shows that Item 2 discriminated perfectly with respect to the criterion. No student who was below criterion on the total test answered this item correctly, and no student above criterion on the total test answered it incorrectly. On the other hand, Item 3 had a negative discrimination index. For some reason, students who were above criterion on the total test did poorly on this item. Such a result should lead to follow-up action by the teachers to determine whether the problem was with the students, the instruction, or, more reasonably, the item. The difficulty levels should also be inspected to check whether they appear to be in the expected range. Readers interested in a more technical development of criterion-referenced item statistics should see *Problems in Criterion-Referenced Measurement* in the references.

SUMMARY

This chapter introduced several measurement and statistical terms. They may be more easily structured in outline form:

    I. Measurement Scales—a continuum indicating the amount of information in a test score.

        A. Nominal

   B. Ordinal
   C. Interval
   D. Ratio

II. Statistics—numbers which describe a set of test scores.
   A. Proportion above criterion
   B. Central tendency
      1. Mean
      2. Median
      3. Mode
   C. Dispersion
      1. Range
      2. Standard Deviation
   D. Correlation

III. Measurement Terms—technical vocabulary of testing.
   A. Reliability
      1. Test-Retest
      2. Alternate Forms
      3. Split-Half
      4. Kuder-Richardson
   B. Validity
      1. Content
      2. Criterion-Related
      3. Construct
   C. Item Analysis
      1. Difficulty
      2. Discrimination

If unit teachers can explain these terms in their own words, they will certainly have the technical vocabulary necessary for constructing, selecting, or evaluating tests to be used when programming instruction for the individual student.

DISCUSSION TOPICS

1. Discuss what information teachers obtain from measures of central tendency and measures of dispersion associated with a distribution of test scores.

2. Describe how correlation might be used in deciding whether or not a mastery performance on one test is necessary before begin-

ning the next unit of study in an academic area. In this kind of situation how are the concepts of prediction being used?

3. Contrast the meanings of reliability and validity of measurement. Describe a situation in which a test might be reliable but lacking in validity.

4. Discuss the information that the difficulty and discrimination indexes provide. What does it mean when an item has negative discrimination power with respect to (1) the scores on the item and (2) possible characteristics of the item? What would it mean if an item had a difficulty index of 1.0?

REFERENCES

Gulliksen, H. 1950. *Theory of mental tests,* New York: Wiley.

Harris, C. W. 1974. Problems of objectives-based measurement in *Problems in criterion-referenced measurement,* CSE Monograph Series in Evaluation, No. 3, Los Angeles: Center for the Study of Evaluation.

Knapp, T. R. 1971. *Statistics for educational measurement,* Scranton: Intext.

Kuder, G. F., and M. W. Richardson 1937. The theory of the estimation of test reliability." *Psychometrika,* 2: 151–160.

Nunnally, J. C. 1967. *Psychometric theory,* New York: McGraw-Hill.

Otto, W., and R. Chester 1976. *Objective-based reading,* Reading, Mass.: Addison-Wesley.

3

Evaluating Student Learning in the Cognitive Domain

Objectives

After reading this chapter, the reader will be able:

- To understand the uses of tests in assessing student learning in the cognitive domain.
- To know sources of tests and test items.
- To understand the uses of observation and work samples in obtaining assessment information in the cognitive domain.
- To comprehend how assessment is based upon instructional objectives.

The majority of instructional objectives for individualizing instruction is concerned with student learning in the skill and academic areas. These are the areas that parents and community most directly associate with student learning. In educational language the skill and academic areas are commonly classified in the cognitive domain.

HIERARCHY OF OBJECTIVES

Evaluation, being a part of instruction, must be referenced to something in instruction, and when programming instruction for the individual student this something is the instructional objective. Therefore, an underlying assumption for evaluation is that the instructional objectives are amenable to evaluation.

Action Verbs in Objectives

It is not a purpose of this text to provide a detailed discussion of the preparation of instructional objectives (see, for example, Nussel, *et al.* 1976). However, in briefly reviewing the components of an instructional objective, a most important component is the verb used in the objective. The verb designates learner, not teacher, behavior.

In order to make objectives amenable to evaluation, action verbs are required. The verb must indicate what the learner will be doing when the objective is being met. In this way, the assessment procedures can directly reflect the verb. For example, the verbs "add, subtract, or square" can be used as action verbs in instructional objectives for mathematics, but a statement such as "to become familiar with" is not adequate for use in an instructional objective. Such statements simply do not indicate what the learner will be doing when the objective is being met, and, therefore, the learner performance cannot be assessed, much less evaluated.

Taxonomy of Objectives

Instructional objectives can be classified into categories which make up a taxonomy. Numerous taxonomies exist. However, one extensively used is that developed by Bloom, *et al.* (1956). This taxonomy contains six major categories in the cognitive domain, and the categories can be considered a hierarchy of learning outcomes. The lowest level or least complex outcome is knowledge, and evaluation is the most complex. The six major categories with descriptive definitions are as follows:

Knowledge: The recall of a wide range of previously learned content, processes, procedures, patterns, structures, etc. Knowledge includes recall of specifics and generalities. However, all that is required is the recall of the information.

Comprehension: The lowest level of understanding. The individual knows what is being communicated and can use the concept or whatever is being communicated. However, use is only direct and does not involve application or relating to other concepts, materials, situations, etc.

Application: The use of learned concepts, etc., in particular and concrete situations. Rules, theories, concepts, methods, etc., are the types of things that are applied.

Analysis: The breakdown of what is communicated (concepts, methods, etc.) into its component parts so that the structure is understood.

Synthesis: The ability to construct parts or elements together to form a whole. Synthesis may require developing a new pattern or structure, or a plan for proceeding.

Evaluation: The ability to judge the value of concepts, materials, procedures, etc., for a specified purpose.

Examples of classifying objectives into this category appear in a later section of this chapter.

A taxonomy can be useful in the preparation of objectives by providing the types of outcomes to be contained in the objectives. If an imbalance exists between the kinds of outcomes in the objectives and what the teachers desire from the learning, this will be indicated. The same kind of classification can be used for the outcomes in assessment items, and an imbalance between outcomes in objectives and items can be detected if such an imbalance exists. This latter type of imbalance is an indication of lack of validity of the assessment items.

USES OF ASSESSMENT INFORMATION IN INSTRUCTIONAL PROGRAMMING FOR THE INDIVIDUAL STUDENT

Assessment information is used for a variety of evaluation purposes but, as was indicated in the first chapter, information is focused basically on two kinds of judgments: What the students are learning, and the effectiveness of the instructional programs. As assessment information is used toward these ends, we can consider the uses of assessment information as being diagnostic, formative, and summative. The uses are differentiated primarily by their purposes, not by unique kinds or forms of information.

Diagnostic Uses

The traditional meaning of a diagnostic test is a test used to identify or analyze a student's specific strengths and weaknesses. Wherever possible, the weaknesses would be corrected and the strengths capitalized on in beginning the next segment of instruction. This general meaning also applies when programming instruction for the individual student. However, the meaning is expanded beyond this traditional meaning of a diagnostic test.

Pretests used to cover short instructional units provide diagnostic information. Pretests are not necessarily tests of the content to be covered, a parallel test to the posttest. Pretests often are used to determine whether or not the student has the prerequisite skills or knowledge necessary for the instruction at hand. For example, suppose an upper elementary or middle school I & R Unit were to have an instructional unit in Introductory Algebra. There would be little point in giving the students a pretest covering the objectives for the algebra instruction. Clearly, the students would not have attained the objectives prior to the instruction. But there are skills and mathematics knowledge that are essential for successfully receiving algebra instruction. The pretest would cover these skills and this knowledge, and diagnose for deficiencies in these prerequisites.

Although we often associate diagnosis as occurring prior to or early in the instruction, it is not so limited. It can also take place while instruction is in progress. For example, responses to subsets of items on a test may be used to diagnose specific kinds of difficulties the student may be having with the content covered by the test. Items so used are called diagnostic item sets.

A diagnostic item set is a set of items that can be scored in such a way that the specific types of student error can be isolated. The first step in constructing a diagnostic item set is to identify the types of errors that are commonly made when learning the content covered by the test. Then options in multiple-choice items are used which are consequences of the errors.

Mathematics is an area in which diagnostic item sets can be effectively used. Suppose that the student is working on dividing by fractions and is taught by applying the "invert and multiply" procedure. Three possible errors in this procedure are:

1. Failure to invert.
2. Inverting the dividend rather than the divisor.
3. Inverting and then adding.

In order to detect these types of errors, example items in an item set might be:

Pretests are often used to determine whether or not students have necessary prerequisite skills for the instruction at hand.

1. $1/2 \div 1/4 =$
   A. 1/8
   B. 1/2
   C. 2
   D. 4 1/2

2. $1/3 \div 2/3 =$
   A. 1 5/6
   B. 1/2
   C. 2/9
   D. 2

3. $3/8 \div 3/4 =$
   A. 1/2
   B. 9/32
   C. 2
   D. 1 17/24

Key: Correct responses C, B, A
       Error No. 1 above A, C, B
       Error No. 2 above B, D, C
       Error No. 3 above D, A, D

Such a scoring key will indicate whether students consistently use an inappropriate procedure for solving these problems. Since diagnostic item sets can be administered in large or small group situations, their use is less time consuming than individualized diagnostic testing and, where appropriate, diagnostic item sets can supplement individualized diagnostic testing.

Published diagnostic tests are available, primarily in the areas of reading and arithmetic. For example, there are "reading readiness" tests which are commonly used at the close of the kindergarten year. Results of these kinds of tests are helpful in diagnosing the student's reading skills so an appropriate instructional program can be developed.

When programming instruction for the individual student, and especially when using the IPM of IGE, other assessment information than test results is used for diagnostic purposes. Information about the learning style and motivation level, for example, of the student is used both for setting instructional objectives and the instructional program for that student. (This is done in Step 3 of the IPM.)

There usually is information about previous student learning evidenced through work samples. Information may be available through observations taken by the teachers. Certainly, the information on the attainment of prerequisite objectives of an instructional unit with an invariant sequence of objectives is helpful for diagnosis. Thus, diagnostic information can and should come from a variety of assessment results.

Formative Uses

While the instructional program for an individual student is being implemented, information is collected for formative purposes. Formative information is used for developing, guiding, or modifying the instructional programs while they are being implemented. This information guides the teachers and the student in making decisions about progress. The daily interaction between the teachers and the student should provide adequate feedback about what the student is accomplishing.

Formative evaluation guards against persisting with inappropriate instruction until some distant terminal point. For example, it may be that the objectives initially set for the student are not realistic. Possibly, the student has not mastered prerequisite objectives and this was not detected when diagnostic information was collected. Adjustments in the learning modes may be in order. Information used in these kinds of ways is being used for formative purposes.

Summative Uses

Summative evaluation is usually associated with that provided at periodic marking occasions or at the close of a particular instructional unit. Summative information can also be helpful to the student and teachers in instructional decision making. It can provide an overall summary or synthesis for the instructional period covered.

Summative evaluation sets the stage for continuing into the next sequence of instruction. In this sense, information collected at a terminal point not only serves summative purposes, but also diagnostic purposes in preparing for the next sequence.

A variety of information such as test scores, work sample results, etc., can be collected for each of the three uses listed above. Since testing is an important function in instructional programming for the individual student, the next several sections of this chapter deal specifically with tests and how they are used. Then later in the chapter, observation and work samples are also discussed as means for obtaining evaluation information in the cognitive domain.

TESTS AND THEIR SOURCES

We usually think of a test as some type of paper-and-pencil stimulus to which the student can respond. However, tests in the cognitive domain could also be administered orally. The remarks that follow, for the most part, also apply to oral tests. In the cognitive domain the items of a test cover a segment of a skills or content area as reflected by the instructional objectives.

Prepared Tests with Curriculum Materials

One source of tests is the published curriculum materials that are available in the academic and skills areas. In order for these materials to be useful when programming instruction for the individual student, the materials must contain instructional objectives. The tests in turn must be criterion-referenced with the criteria being established within, or supplemental to, the objectives.

Published curriculum materials that include tests often provide the option to use some tests as pretests and others as posttests. An instructional unit will likely contain the instructional objectives, suggestions for activities, and two or more tests covering the objectives of the unit. Published tests are also easy to obtain. Most published tests are technically well constructed. These are the advantages of using tests that are commercially prepared with published curriculum materials.

Available Items

Attractive as tests with published curriculum materials may appear, they have certain disadvantages when programming instruction for the individual student. An entire test may not be applicable for the objectives of a specific student. As the student is progressing through an instructional unit which has a variable sequence for attaining the objectives, the tests may not correspond well with the sequence. Published tests find their greatest use with common objectives that are attained in an invariant sequence.

Rather than placing individual items into test format, some publishers provide pools or sets of possible items that are referenced to the given instructional objectives. The obvious advantage of item pools is that the items can be selected for their relationship to specific objectives and then assembled into tests. In this way it is much easier to assemble a test appropriate for the instructional program of a specific student than when entire tests must be used.

There have been attempts to package criterion-referenced tests which are independent of specific curriculum materials. In some cases the packages also contain instructional objectives. The tests or items are then referenced back to the objectives. An example of such a package is the *Prescriptive Mathematics Inventory* (PMI) published by the California Test Bureau—McGraw-Hill. The PMI was designed to measure 351 objectives representing mathematics taught in the intermediate and upper elementory levels.

The test items from criterion-referenced testing packages such as the PMI are a useful source of items if they apply to the instructional objectives selected for a student. Since they are not related to specific curriculum materials, they are useful for assessing general skills and knowledge in the academic areas.

Teacher-constructed Items

Published tests and items are very helpful for assessing student learning, but often evaluation using published items is supplemented by teacher-constructed items and tests. When programming instruction for the individual student, the flexibility of using teacher-constructed tests should be retained. This is so even if curriculum programs with specified tests and classroom management systems are used.

We do not intend to describe procedures for constructing items. However, we can briefly consider three example objectives and the behaviors that a student would demonstrate to provide evidence of the student's having met the objectives. The expected behaviors must be kept in mind when constructing test items.

The sample objectives (Toledo Diocesan Schools 1972) are taken from intermediate level social studies instruction and are in a single grouping:

1. The student will present five reasons for the development of cities in the past. All reasons will be provided in acceptable form.

Specific behaviors: (1a) Writes one or more reasons. ·

(1b) Selects reasons from a larger listing of reasons.

(1c) Matches the reasons to the concept of city development.

2. The student will give one example of a city that began as (1) a trade center, (2) a government center, (3) a fort (protection), (4) a business center (manufacturing). Examples will be given with 100 percent accuracy.

Specific behaviors: (2a) Writes the names of the cities.

(2b) Distinguishes between cities as to their purpose of origin.

(2c) Matches city to purpose of origin.

(2d) Identifies cities that fit a given purpose of origin.

3. The student will locate ten cities on a map and designate their purposes of origin as one of the four listed in the preceding objective. Acceptable performance will be 80 percent accuracy.

Specific behaviors: (3a) Identifies cities correctly on a map.

(3b) Shown specific cities on the map, writes their purpose of origin.

(3c) Infers the purpose of origin of cities on a hypothetical map.

(3d) Selects on hypothetical maps cities that are trading centers because of their locations.

For the most part, the three objectives listed above imply knowledge, comprehension, and application level outcomes when classified using Bloom's taxonomy. Specific behavior 3c and possibly 3b might involve analyses level outcomes. The specific behaviors listed could be the basis for constructing test items. Many types of items could be used to have the student demonstrate the behaviors.

PLANNING THE TEST

If tests published with curriculum materials are used, it is not necessary to plan the test, but there should be some planning on the timing of the test. Tests, of course, should be administered after the instruction for the objectives. Curriculum materials often suggest appropriate testing times in the teacher's manual.

When programming instruction for the individual student, testing involves using the objectives as a basis for interpreting results. Therefore, it is necessary to group objectives and, through them, instructional content for testing purposes. Rarely would a test be devoted entirely to a single instructional objective. If such were the case, the student would be on a perpetual merry-go-round of testing. Therefore, one of the first steps in planning a test is to group or assemble those instructional objectives that are to be covered by the test.

Since instructional objectives are usually prepared in groups covering units of instruction or some kind of grouping of instructional content, the same groupings can be used for preparing tests. In an IGE school the I & R Unit staff decides upon the frequency of testing. A test may cover three weeks of instruction devoted to a single, general topic. Groupings of objectives would tend to be within skills or subject areas, but this is not a requirement. It may be desirable to cover instruction from two or more skills or subject areas with a single test.

Once the list of objectives to be covered by the test is developed, specific student behaviors can be identified for each objective. These are the behaviors that a student would demonstrate as evidence of meeting the objective. Examples of such behaviors were given with the three social studies objectives listed earlier.

PUTTING THE TEST TOGETHER

Identifying items for each objective does not complete the planning or preparation of the test. For one thing, an imbalance can be created because objectives for which it is easy to generate items may be over-represented. One way to guard against this situation is to prepare a "Table of Specifications" for the test. A table of specifications is a two-dimensional grid (Gronlund 1973, pp. 26–27) containing numbers of items in its cells. One dimension of the grid contains the instructional objectives or, if a great deal of detail was required, the specific behaviors could be listed on that dimension. The other dimension contains the subject or skills (content) areas to be covered by the test. The topical indentification of the content to be covered is usually quite straightforward. The designation of the numbers of items would be based on factors such as the relevant importance of the objectives and/or the amount of instructional time devoted to each. The use of a Table of Specifications aids in establishing content validity for the test.

In planning the test the teachers should have an accurate estimate of the length of a test, say 40 objective-type items. Then the cell numbers can be completed and the marginal totals will indicate the number of items devoted to objectives and content.

An example of a Table of Specifications is presented in Table 3.1. Note that numbers of items for objectives (or content) are not equal. For example, Objective 4 receives twice the number of items that Objective 3 receives.

Table 3.1 An example table of specifications for a 20-item test on social studies.

Content	Objective 1	2	3	4	5	Total
Development of cities	2	1	1	1	1	6
Characteristics of cities	1	1	1	3	1	7
Governance of cities	1	2	1	2	1	7
Total	4	4	3	6	3	20

The extent to which the content is divided into topics is basically an arbitrary decision of the teachers planning the test. Whatever specificity or breakdown is most helpful should be used. When planning tests that cover large instructional periods, for example, nine weeks or a semester, teachers may want to use the more general educational objectives rather than instructional objectives. Otherwise, the table may contain so many cells that it becomes cumbersome.

At this point let us briefly consider some factors relevant to assembling a test.

Relative Numbers of Items

We have already alluded to the relative importance of the objectives in influencing the numbers of items in the cells of the table. The number of items is also influenced by the seriousness of making an interpretation error. An interpretation error would be inferring that a student has mastered an objective when the student has not, or vice versa. For those objectives for which an error would be more serious, a larger sampling of items would be provided. The time available for testing, of course, influences the total number of items of the test.

With criterion-referenced tests, current practice seems to favor three to five items per objective (Klien and Kosecoff 1973). This seems to be based more on practicality and feasibility than educational or testing theory.

As the length of a test is increased by the addition of similar items, the reliability of the test is also increased. Logically, increased test length will have the effect of reducing errors in the sampling of content; that is, content sampling will tend to be enhanced. Also, errors due to fluctuations in the individual will tend to be reduced. These are the kinds of errors that reduce reliability.

It is relatively easy to estimate the reliability of a test of increased length if we know the reliability of the original test. The formula for the reliability of the longer test is given by:

$$r_\mathrm{m} = \frac{kr_\mathrm{o}}{1 + (k-1)r_\mathrm{o}}$$

in which r_o = reliability of the original test,
r_m = reliability of the longer test,
k = factor of increase.*

Consider an example of how much reliability may be increased by increased length. Suppose an original test of ten items had a reliability of 0.80 and the test were increased to twenty items; that is, $k = 2$ because the new test would be twice as long as the original. The reliability of the 20-item test would be given by:

$$r_\mathrm{m} = \frac{2(0.8)}{1 + (2-1)(0.8)} = 0.88.$$

Thus, doubling the length increases the test reliability in this case by 0.08. If tests are quite short and tend to have low reliabilities, increasing their lengths (probably as much as by three or four times) may be considered. The increased testing time will also need to be considered before lengthening tests.

Item Formats

Teachers have available for paper-and-pencil tests a variety of item formats such as multiple-choice, matching, completion, and essay.

---

*   Note: k is *not* the number of items added but the factor by which the test is lengthened. For example, if a test were lengthened from 10 to 15 items, k would equal $3/2$.

With criterion-referenced testing, objective-type items such as multiple-choice tend to be used more than essay items.

For test scoring it is often more convenient to use a single format only. However, in order to cover adequately certain objectives it may be best to use different formats, for example, both matching and multiple-choice. It may even be desirable to vary the mode of presentation and response. For example, a written test could be supplemented with orally administered items. If teachers are to construct items, they should decide at the planning stage on the item formats to be used.

Grouping Items in the Test

With criterion-referenced testing, the grouping of items within the test should be done by instructional objective. With that condition met, to the extent possible, items should be arranged from easy to difficult. If the test contains two or more sections, such arrangement would of necessity need to be within sections. Sometimes items in the same format are grouped in one section. Explicit and understandable directions should be provided for the test and for each section if there are different sections. Items should be arranged so that they are easy to read, easy to respond to, and easy to score. Items should be consecutively numbered. When machine-scored answer sheets are used, it is usually necessary to continue the numbering of items across the sections of the test.

Using a Test for Objectives—An Example

Thus far, this discussion has centered primarily on how to obtain test items and how to put together a test. At this point, a science example is presented that includes objectives and test items related to the objectives. The example is taken from *Science—A Process Approach* which was produced by the American Association for the Advancement of Science/Xerox Corporation.* All science examples presented in this chapter are taken from this work. This particular example is taken from curriculum materials appropriate for the intermediate level.

---

* The copyrights for the experimental and revised editions were held by the American Association for the Advancement of Science. However, as stated in the materials, after September 1, 1974, no copyright shall subsist or be claimed in this work. Copies of this work or portions thereof may be made after March 1, 1974, provided that no publication, sale, or distribution of any such copies is made until after September 1, 1974.

The instructional unit is entitled "Defining Operationally Electric Circuits and Their Parts." The following three objectives are listed and on the right side of the listing is provided the classification of the objectives (outcomes) in Bloom's taxonomy (the classification is that of the authors).

Objectives	*Taxonomy classification*
At the end of this exercise the child should be able to:	
1. *Identify* an object, a situation, or an event which is related to simple electric circuits and is described by an operational definition.	1. Knowledge
2. *Distinguish* between an operational and a nonoperational definition of an object, a situation, or an event related to simple electric circuits.	2. Comprehension
3. *Construct* a simple electric circuit from an operational definition.	3. Application (possibly synthesis with a complex item or task)

Since this example will use a set of published items for the test, the taxonomy classifications of the learning outcomes implied by the objectives are not used in assembling a test. However, the classification does illustrate the hierarchy of the taxonomy and the specific levels that include these objectives.

It should be noted that as stated above the objectives do not contain explicit criteria for their attainment. The behaviors indicated in the objectives must be demonstrated, so in essence there is a 100 percent correct criterion. However, as will be seen in the items, which are called tasks, the acceptable behavior (which is the criterion) is indicated for each task. (This format also applies to later science examples.)

The student participates in various learning activities using appropriate materials in an attempt to meet the objectives. These learning activities are described in the materials. After the appropriate instruction the student is administered the following three items (tasks):

INDIVIDUAL COMPETENCY MEASURE

(Individual score sheets for each pupil are in the Teacher Drawer.)

TASK 1 (OBJECTIVE 2): Give the child the data sheet (see Figure 14) and refer to the illustrations. Say, **On this page are three definitions of a thermostat. After I read the definitions with you, put "X" beside the one that is the best operational definition.** Read the definitions with the child.

_____A. **A thermostat is a kind of switch that is part of an electric circuit in houses, cars, and refrigerators.**

_____B. **A thermostat is an electric switch that is changed from a nonconductor to a conductor by temperature changes.**

_____C. **A thermostat is a safety device used to keep things from getting too hot or too cold.**

Acceptable Behavior

The child selects B.

TASK 2, 3 (OBJECTIVES 1 AND 3): Say, **Next on the data sheet is an operational definition of a potentiometer.** (Point to the definition and read it with the child.) **A potentiometer is a device which, when connected in the circuit shown below, changes the brightness of the lamp gradually. The brightness of the lamp is changed by rotating the knob.** Give the child the materials with which to construct the circuit and two similar devices with two terminals and a knob. One of these should be a potentiometer and the other a rotary switch. Say, **Here are two devices. Connect the circuit, and use the operational definition to decide which device is a potentiometer.**

Acceptable Behavior

For Task 2, the child correctly assembles the circuit; for Task 3, he correctly identifies the potentiometer.

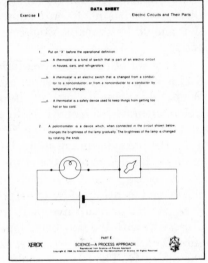

FIGURE 14

The three items above make up what is called an "Individual Competency Measure." The items can be administered individually to the student as indicated; an oral presentation with a written response. It would also be possible to present these items in a written mode with appropriate adjustments in the directions. If, for example, these items were to be included in a longer test covering two or more units, the latter approach would be used. In this sense, the items provide excellent flexibility of use when programming instruction for the individual student.

Interpreting Test Results—The Example Continued

The items or tasks described above specified the acceptable behavior for having completed the task and thus provided evidence for having attained the objective. (Note that each task is referenced to one of the three objectives.) If a student does the three items correctly, the objectives have been attained. This interpretation of the result is straightforward and unambiguous. It is decided that the student is ready to begin the next unit in this sequence of science units (summative evaluation).

Suppose the student does not provide acceptable behavior for all of the items; say Item 3 is missed. The initial interpretation is that Objective 3 has not been attained. However, additional information that should be available would now be used in deciding on a course of action.

This set of curriculum materials has sequenced units, thus establishing a hierarchy of dependencies among the objectives across units. What this means is that certain objectives are prerequisite to others. Behaviors have been analyzed to determine the subordinate behaviors that the student should have acquired before being expected to acquire the behavior in question. The behaviors of these items have subordinate behaviors that the student should have acquired earlier.

A record is kept on the "Competency Measure Score Sheet" of the behaviors attained by the student in sequence. Obviously, the student should have attained subordinate behaviors before attempting objectives with the new behaviors. But, it is possible that one or more subordinate behaviors were not adequately acquired, and therein lies the difficulty. The student could be retested or rechecked on subordinate behaviors (diagnostic evaluation).

If all subordinate behaviors seem to be intact, a review of the learning activities that relate to Objective 3 is in order. Information on the student's motivation level and preferred learning style could be used in restructuring learning activities in an attempt to attain the objective. Possibly, the student had been working in a small group on constructing circuits and now some individual activity would be helpful. The teacher's judgment is involved, and this is part of the evaluation process (formative evaluation).

This particular example necessarily has a limited number of objectives and items. Teachers might want to identify or construct two or more items for one objective, especially if a summative evaluation covering an extensive period is involved. Then a percentage correct criterion, for example, 80 percent correct, would likely be used as an indication of having attained the objective. Performance on the items should be referenced back to the individual objectives, however, since it is the objectives on which instruction, and hence evaluation, is based.

OBSERVATION AND WORK SAMPLES

Testing is by no means the only method for evaluating student learning in the cognitive domain. A good deal of information is obtained through the daily contact between students and teachers. Such information is collected primarily through two nontesting methods: observation and work samples. These two methods are exactly what the names imply. Teachers obtain observational information by watching students engaged in activities or tasks, either individually or collectively. Observation is important at all levels of the elementary school, but it is especially important at the primary level since the number of writing activities at this level is limited.

A work sample is a nontest product of student learning. Samples might represent any number of products—handwriting, spelling, drawing, report preparation, problem solutions, science projects, etc. Work samples may often be written, although nonwritten work samples can also be assessed.

When nonwritten work samples are used, the distinction between observation and work sample is not always definitive and the two methods may overlap. Examples of nonwritten work samples include oral reading and demonstrating a science experiment. For the latter, a student would be observed while conducting the experiment (observation) and the result of the experiment may be some product (work sample) that could also be assessed.

Observation—A Science Example

The example below is taken from an instructional unit entitled "Describing Changes in Plants" which is part of the *Science—A Process Approach* curriculum materials. The unit is appropriate for the primary level.

Objectives	*Taxonomy classification*
The objectives for this unit are: (Taxonomy classifications are also given.)	
1. *Identify* and *name* observed changes in a plant.	1. Knowledge

APPRAISAL

Pack soil or wads of paper toweling around the stem of a coleus, tomato, geranium, or other large potted plant until the pot is filled from the soil surface up to its rim. Cover the top of the pot around the stem of the plant with a piece of plastic film so that the contents of the pot will not fall out when the plant is inverted.

In a closet or cabinet which can be darkened, arrange two boxes or piles of books so the plant can be suspended in an inverted position between them, with the rim of the pot resting on the boxes or books. (See Figure 2.) Ask one child at a time to describe the plant's arrangement and appearance. Repeat the observation and communication at intervals during the day—and the following day or two—until the tip of the plant has curved and is growing upward. Except when the children are observing it, the plant should remain in the dark. If necessary, you can add water to the soil by dripping it through the drainage hole in the "top" of the pot.

Each child's description should include some of the following observations: the direction of the stem's orientation, any changes in the position of the leaves, the curvature of the stem and leaves, a comparison of the plant with earlier descriptions, statements describing the speed of the changes, and color changes of the plant's growing portions. After one child has described the plant, call on other children to describe their observations, or to double-check the statements of the first observer. Repeat this procedure at intervals as changes occur, so that most of the class will have an opportunity to demonstrate their ability to communicate observations.

COMPETENCY MEASURE

(Individual score sheets for each pupil are in the Teacher Drawer.)
TASK 1 (OBJECTIVES 1-3): Show the child the row of drawings marked (A) on the chart. (See Figure 3.) Fold the sheet, or cover part of it with a blank sheet of paper, so that the row of drawings marked (B) is not now visible. Say, **These are drawings of a single plant which was moved into a dark room. The room had only one window which was covered with a shade. On the first day, the shade was raised to let the light in** (point to the window), **and the plant looked like this** (point). **On the second day it looked like this** (point). **On the third day, like this** (point), **and on the fourth day, like this** (point). **Describe what happened to the plant. What changes took place in the four days?**

Put one check in the acceptable column if he gives a description which says that the plant was erect on the first day, that its leaves turned toward the light next, and that its stem and leaves then moved in the same direction.

TASK 2 (OBJECTIVE 4): Show the child both of the rows of drawings, (A) and (B), and say, **Here are the drawings of another plant, besides the first one. What is the difference between the changes that are taking place in these two plants** (designate them) **from day to day?**

Put one check in the acceptable column if the child says that Plant B is changing faster, or that its response to the light is greater.

FIGURE 2

FIGURE 3

SCIENCE—A PROCESS APPROACH/PART B
American Association for the Advancement of Science/XEROX Corporation

20227-18

2. *Describe* what was done to produce the observed changes.

2. Knowledge

3. *Describe* the order in which the observed changes occurred.

3. Comprehension

4. *Describe* the direction of motion and the rate of change of the motion of the parts of the plant which responded to the stimulus.

4. Comprehension

The appraisal activity and the competency measure are provided on the preceding page as they appear in the curriculum materials. The appraisal activity provides observational data. The teacher observes and records the student's reaction to and description of what is happening to the plant. Note that, in the appraisal activity as well as in the competency measure, definite criteria are indicated for the student's behavior. A check on the student's individual score sheet represents acceptable demonstration of competency.

The competency measure could be considered an oral test or it might be a nonwritten work sample. If it is used as the summative assessment for the instructional unit, it would likely be considered a test. Note that in all of this assessment the student responds individually and is assessed individually. If the student does not provide the acceptable responses, instructional activities covering the content of the unit are provided in the curriculum materials.

Work Sample—A Science Example

The following example is taken from the same curriculum materials as the preceding example, and it is from the intermediate level. The activity described below relates to the following three objectives:

Objectives

Taxonomy classification

1. *Construct* a complete electric circuit consisting of a flashlight cell, a lamp, and two wires.

1. Application

2. *Construct* inferred connection patterns for hidden circuits.

2. Analysis

3. *Describe* the expected outcomes of future tests based upon inferred connection patterns.

3. Comprehension

Activity 3—Inferring Connection Patterns Among Six Points

Give each pair of children the circuit test equipment shown in Figure 6, two of the eight circuit boards whose wiring patterns are shown below (see Figure 11), and two copies of the data-sheet, *Inferring Connection Patterns Among Six Points*. (See Figure 12.)

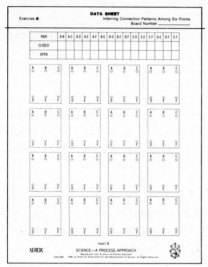

FIGURE 11

FIGURE 12

Tell the children to use the dry cell and the lamp circuit to determine which pairs of points can be touched to make a closed circuit. They should identify the number of the board, and record it along with their observations on their data sheets as in *Activity 2*.

After the children have completed the testing procedure, ask them to infer connection patterns and to sketch possible ways of connecting the wires between the labeled points. Tell them to sketch several connection patterns for any board which could possibly have more than one. Only one inferred connection pattern is possible for Circuit Boards No. 1, 2, 3, 4, and 8. Sixteen inferred patterns are possible for No. 5; four are possible for No. 6. A great many possibilities exist for No. 7.

Figure 13 shows the connection patterns the children should infer, except that none of the many possibilities is shown for Board No. 7.

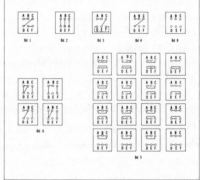

FIGURE 13

Figure 6 which is referred to in the description of the activity is simply the figure of a dry cell and lamp circuit. (It appears earlier in the materials.) It is suggested that students work in pairs; however, the teachers could have students working individually. Figure 12 contains the student worksheet which, when completed, becomes the product or work sample. Figure 13 shows the correct connection patterns for the exercise.

There is no definite criteria for performance on the work sample specified in the materials. Teachers can specify criteria or provide percentage correct scores. This is an activity which takes place within the instruction, and it is not used for summative evaluation of student learning for the instructional unit. The information would be used for formative evaluation to determine whether or not additional instruction is needed for the student on these connecting patterns.

Written Report as a Work Sample

Occasionally in areas such as social studies and science, the student is required to prepare a report of several pages on a single topic. The report might deal with a country or industry, for example. An extensive report of this nature would require student behaviors that relate to several objectives. Language arts skills are required as well as knowledge and comprehension of the topic. Synthesis behaviors may be required in order to pull the report together. In evaluating this type of report a list of criteria might well be used, such a list having been developed prior to evaluating any reports. The criteria should be established by the unit teachers, and the students should be explicitly informed as to what is expected of them. There should be no mystery about the nature of the criteria.

The criteria by which a report is evaluated may vary somewhat depending upon the objectives which the report is designed to meet. However, there are criteria of organization, neatness, correct spelling, and correct sentence structure that are relevant to practically any report. Additional criteria might be used in a combination such as:

1. Inclusion of relevant points.
2. Comprehensiveness of the coverage of the topic.
3. Continuity of the ideas in the report.
4. Relating the major points in the report.
5. Recognizing major and minor points.

It may be desirable for teachers to sample pages from each report and very carefully check routine things such as spelling and punctuation. Of course, the entire report will need to be read for content.

It is not feasible to include in this text an entire report as an example work sample. However, Figure 3.1 contains a sample page from a report on woodland animals. This page is from a report prepared by a student in an intermediate unit of an IGE school.

The criteria by which a report or a page from a report is evaluated are important, but it is very unlikely they would result in a mastery-nonmastery dichotomy of evaluation. For example, consider the criteria of "having correct punctuation." Teachers could identify punctuation errors and such errors could be counted, but it is not likely that a criterion such as, "fewer than six punctuation errors in a report indicates mastery of punctuation skills," would be used. Rather the criterion of "correct punctuation" is used as a direction in which we desire the students to go. If a student had previously been making an excessive number of punctuation errors and in the report had reduced

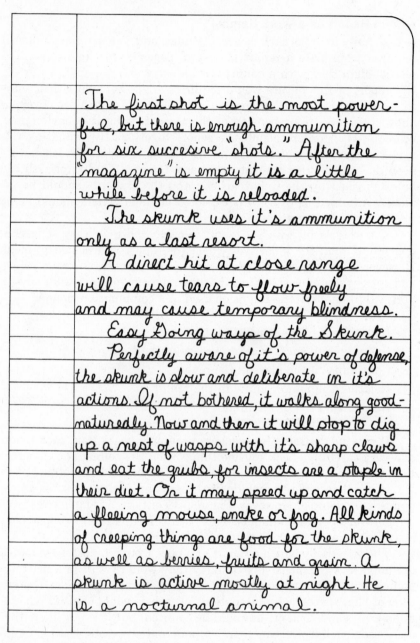

The first shot is the most powerful, but there is enough ammunition for six successive "shots." After the "magazine" is empty it is a little while before it is reloaded.

The skunk uses it's ammunition only as a last resort.

A direct hit at close range will cause tears to flow freely and may cause temporary blindness.

Easy Going ways of the Skunk.

Perfectly aware of it's power of defense, the skunk is slow and deliberate in it's actions. If not bothered, it walks along good-naturedly. Now and then it will stop to dig up a nest of wasps, with it's sharp claws and eat the grubs, for insects are a staple in their diet. Or it may speed up and catch a fleeing mouse, snake or frog. All kinds of creeping things are food for the skunk, as well as berries, fruits and grain. A skunk is active mostly at night. He is a nocturnal animal.

Fig. 3.1   A written work sample from a report on woodland animals.

Performance when participating in a science experiment is an example of a nonwritten work sample.

this number, progress is being made toward attaining the criterion. But without having perfect punctuation the student would not be considered a mastery writer.

The primary value of evaluation of a work sample such as the one illustrated lies in the learning experience it provides for the student. Hopefully, the learning experience is not terminated when the report is handed in. The teacher can identify for the student where errors have been made, and also discuss how errors would be corrected. The student and teacher should have a discussion of how sentence structure, for example, might have been improved at certain points. But, it is important that the teacher not concentrate entirely on the errors or weak points of the report. Evaluation should emphasize the strong points as well and the child should be praised for the well-done parts or characteristics of the report.

SUMMARY

This chapter has emphasized ways of evaluating student learning when programming instruction for the individual student. Evaluation must be directed toward ascertaining whether or not the instructional objectives have been met by the student. Evaluation, being a part of instruction, is objectives-based.

The teacher has available several sources of tests and items—intact tests with published curriculum materials, selection of published items, or teacher-constructed items. Illustrations were provided in this chapter, but compendiums of tests or items should be obtained from materials dealing with specific academic and skills areas.

The teacher should be cognizant of the different categories of the taxonomy for objectives in the cognitive domain. This hierarchical classification system can be helpful when assembling tests to ensure that the items properly represent the desired learning outcomes. A table of specifications was suggested for helping ensure the content validity of the test.

The latter part of the chapter dealt with examples of assessment information obtained through testing, observation, and work samples. Examples illustrated a variety of assessment information dealing with student learning. It is important to note that in all cases instructional objectives set the stage for the evaluation.

DISCUSSION TOPICS

1. Discuss why considering objectives in a hierarchy (with respect to the learning outcomes they contain) is helpful in assembling or constructing tests.

2. Identify a set of published curriculum materials with tests or items included in an area of your interest. Consider whether the test items are closely tied to the objectives. Discuss the adequacy of the published test or items when assessing student learning of the individual student.

3. Discuss the importance of using information from observation and work samples as well as test information when evaluating student learning. Describe observation and work samples that might be used with the curriculum materials identified in (2) above.

REFERENCES

Bloom, B., *et al.* 1956. *Taxonomy of educational objectives: the classification of educational goals.* Handbook I, Cognitive Domain. New York: McKay.

Gronlund, N. 1973. *Preparing criterion-referenced tests for classroom instruction.* New York: Macmillan.

Klein, S. P., and J. Kosecoff 1973. Issues and procedures in the development of criterion-referenced tests, *TM Report 26.*

Nussel, E., J. Inglis, and W. Wiersma 1976. *The teacher and individually guided education.* Reading, Mass.: Addison-Wesley.

Toledo Diocesan Schools, 1972. *Curriculum guide for elementary school social studies.* Toledo, Ohio.

4
Evaluating Student Learning in the Affective and Psychomotor Domains

Objectives

- After reading this chapter the reader will be able:
- To differentiate among cognitive, affective, and psychomotor variables.
- To understand how affective and psychomotor evaluation fit into instructional programming for the individual student.
- To construct rating scales and checklists.
- To distinguish between paper-and-pencil and observational assessment of affective and psychomotor variables.

It is important to measure student outcomes in the affective and psychomotor domains as well as the traditionally measured cognitive outcomes. A burgeoning awareness of these variables is evidenced in new programs such as *Individually Guided Motivation* (Klausmeier *et al.*, 1972). The purpose of this chapter is to provide for the reader an awareness of some techniques for including these variables in the evaluation of student progress and in the evaluation of the instructional program.

MEASURING AFFECTIVE VARIABLES

The attitudes, feelings, and opinions of students and teachers need to be considered as critical variables in evaluating the effectiveness of the instructional program. Affective variables are quite different from cognitive variables though, in one important respect. The indirectness of affective measures leads often to measurement instruments that are transparent; that is, the preferred response is too obvious, or the measured behaviors are not really an adequate definition of the variable to be measured.

The desired behavior and the measurement are closely linked in the cognitive domain. An objective in mathematics might be concerned with solving inequalities. The test of that objective would require the student to solve inequalities. In contrast, an affective objective may deal with students' attitudes toward mathematics as measured by a questionnaire. The questionnaire is more of an indirect, remote measure of attitude which is hoped to be related to student attitude. It is the extra link between what is said and what is done that provides an opportunity for slippage that does not occur when measuring the attainment of cognitive objectives.

Nonetheless, it is desirable to include affective measures as part of the total assessment program. These measures can be taken as one additional source of data which provides a different perspective for evaluating the effects of the instructional programs. For example, when students are mastering the cognitive objectives satisfactorily, instructional means may be so forceful as to "turn off" the students. This situation could be a problem in the long run. Assessment that includes both cognitive and affective measures would keep teachers aware of such situations.

Affective Measures and Instructional Programming for the Individual Student

Some affective measures will be directly linked to affective objectives and, as such, will relate to instructional programming for the individual student in the same way that the cognitive objectives did in

Student attitudes are important variables in the effectiveness
of instructional programs.

Chapter 3. However, most of the affective measures will be used at
the following step in such instructional programming:

> Assess the level of achievement, learning style, and motivation
> level of each student by use of criterion-referenced tests, observation
> schedules, and work samples with appropriate-sized subgroups.

The data obtained at this step are used as the basis of decisions
about specific objectives for individual students. It is very important
that all the relevant data are used. Teachers need to know which objectives the student has recently mastered, attitudes toward particular instructional strategies, and which other students in the unit
might work cooperatively with the student. Some of these data will be
gathered informally in the discussions among the teachers, but the
data from the students themselves should be gathered in a systematic
manner so that consistent interpretations can be made.

Affective Objectives

The unit staff may choose to set some affective objectives for students. Such objectives might possibly deal with student attitudes,
student interests, and student characteristics such as independence,

motivation, or maturity. A distinction that must be mentioned which contrasts these objectives with cognitive objectives is the whole issue of student accountability. A student can be considered to be failing if that student rarely masters a cognitive objective or proceeds through the sequence of objectives at an extremely slow pace. However, if a student does not achieve criterion on an affective objective, who is at fault? The degree of student responsibility is clearly different on this kind of objective. Thus we can conclude that affective objectives play an important role in the instructional program but they cannot be considered to be the same as cognitive objectives.

Taxonomy of Affective Objectives

A useful taxonomy of objectives in the affective domain was produced by Krathwohl *et al.* (1964). This taxonomy was intended to be hierarchical and reflect the degree to which a concept is internalized. Figure 4.1 depicts the Krathwohl taxonomy.

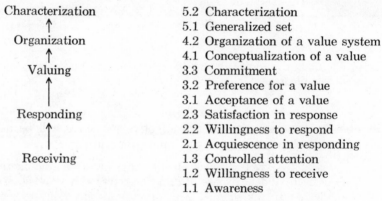

Characterization

↑

Organization

↑

Valuing

↑

Responding

↑

Receiving

5.2 Characterization
5.1 Generalized set
4.2 Organization of a value system
4.1 Conceptualization of a value
3.3 Commitment
3.2 Preference for a value
3.1 Acceptance of a value
2.3 Satisfaction in response
2.2 Willingness to respond
2.1 Acquiescence in responding
1.3 Controlled attention
1.2 Willingness to receive
1.1 Awareness

Fig. 4.1 The taxonomy of educational objectives in the affective domain.

Perhaps an example of an affective objective in a primary unit would illustrate the Krathwohl taxonomy. Suppose that Janet, a seven-year-old student, has not mastered an objective in mathematics for two weeks. The teachers talk to Janet about the lack of progress and find that the reason for the neglected math objectives was that Janet has been spending most of her time on a science project about weather. She has worked independently on this project and is doing a fine job.

In their discussion with Janet they note that she has implied that the math objectives just do not seem important to her now that she is so taken with her independent science project. The teachers decide at this point that they should set an objective that would deal with developing an appreciation for the role of mathematics in science. If Janet were to master such an objective, she might do better in both science and math.

In the terms of the Krathwohl taxonomy there are several levels of internalization that might be selected. The teachers must decide which level is appropriate for Janet. The lowest level, receiving, assesses one's awareness of and attention to the concept. The student might be at this level when she realizes that numbers are used extensively in science.

The second level, responding, includes willingness and satisfaction in responding. Janet would be at this level when she realizes that numbers are the language of science, and she uses numbers to explain scientific principles. The valuing level would perhaps be reached when she regards nonempirical arguments as not very scientific. Organization would occur when the role of mathematics in science is integrated into one's value system—hardly an expectation for a seven-year-old like Janet. Characterization would imply a commitment and understanding similar to the ideals of scientists and mathematicians.

The teachers would most likely set at least a responding level objective where Janet might appreciate the interdependence of mathematics and science. An example objective for Janet would be:

> The student will demonstrate an appreciation for the role of mathematics in science by using numerical examples in at least five of six explanations of scientific phenomena.

The teacher could then have Janet explain some of the terms and principles from her science project to determine whether she does appreciate the interdependence. If she does, this information could serve as a motivator for progress on the math objectives. If she does not meet the criterion, the teachers would take appropriate action in the instructional programming for Janet such as structuring some integrated math and science activities.

Questionnaires and Rating Scales

Affective objectives are typically assessed by paper-and-pencil devices such as questionnaires and rating scales or by direct observation of student behavior. The paper-and-pencil measures, of course, cannot be used with very young children, but some yes-no questions can be administered orally, especially to nonreaders. The observation techniques, however, can be used at all levels.

Questionnaires and self-report rating scales that measure affective variables are usually constructed by teachers to assess the major indicators of student performance. This task is not formidable if a few common sense rules are followed:

1. Keep items homogeneous. When items over a broad range of topics are used, a single score conceals more than it reveals. Different aspects are summed together and the score becomes difficult to interpret.

2. Allow for directionality. It would be a mistake to use items like "I enjoy reading _____ always, _____ sometimes." This item does not allow a negative response. The results might be erroneously interpreted as showing a positive attitude toward reading when the questions have actually determined the outcome.

3. Indicate the intensity. When the number of possible responses is too restricted there can be a real loss of information. For example, a yes-no answer key does not discriminate between those who are moderately committed and those who are strongly committed. Hence, a five-point scale is often preferred to a two- or three-point scale.

4. Avoid vagueness. It is important that the words mean the same thing to all respondents. Any ambiguity results in students responding to items that are perceived differently, and then their responses are not comparable.

5. Avoid emotional terms. Labeling something as either "old-fashioned" or "innovative" would clearly show which response is more socially desirable.

Following the rules above will not ensure valid and reliable scales but disregarding them will surely result in inadequate measurement instruments.

Building Rating Scales and Checklists

The best method for building affective measures is to use much the same procedure as was used in developing cognitive measures. That is, explicitly state the objectives in terms of specific student behaviors. Then the assessment device will be implied by the objectives. For example, the objective "the student will enjoy reading" might better be stated as:

> Given a choice of free time activities, the student will choose independent reading at least twice a week.

or

The student will respond positively to at least 80 percent of the statements on an attitude toward reading questionnaire.

In these latter cases the word "enjoy" has been defined in terms of observable outcomes. The ambiguity of the verb in the objective has been eliminated.

Operational definition of affective behaviors. It should be clear from this example that there are many possible operational definitions for the vague affective terms *enjoy, appreciate,* etc. The translation into observable student outcomes is not nearly as direct as it was in the cognitive domain. For this reason it can be quite useful to include more than one specific affective objective in an area. For example, a general objective which deals with student enjoyment of reading could be translated into several specific objectives which call for a variety of assessment procedures. This is useful because any one operational definition of "enjoying reading" would probably be inadequate.

Example rating scales in mathematics. Once the list of desirable student behaviors is specified in the objectives, it may be necessary to translate behaviors into rating scales so that students can respond to them. The goal should be clarity of thought and ease of responding. The questions should be straightforward and easy to mark. Trick questions and subtle shades of meaning will probably confuse the respondents rather than tease information from them. Some example items from two scales measuring attitudes toward mathematics are presented in Figures 4.2 and 4.3. These items were designed for primary and middle school students, respectively. The complete scales contain about twenty items.

The SMILE scale (Figure 4.2) contains brief, clear statements (Kish 1973). The means for responding are nonthreatening and easily understood. Students get one point for each preferred response on the mathematics items and one total scale is reported. The two-choice answer format is used because of the age of the students tested. Finer discrimination is sacrificed to gain ease of responding.

The middle school measure (Figure 4.3) contains items drawn from the literature on attitudes toward mathematics (Hering 1973). Four factors are measured by the one instrument so either the four separate scores or the one total score could be reported. The intensity and directionality of feelings are assessed using five-point scales. Scores on the separate items can be summed if one is willing to assume equal intervals between adjacent options. That is, the psychological distance between "Strongly Agree" and "Agree" (1 to 2) is

Student Interest Inventory, Grades 1—3

Directions:

Draw the mouth in the face
to show how you feel when
you do the following activities

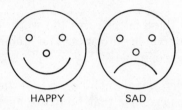

HAPPY   SAD

Samples:

How do you feel when you

a. go to an ice cream store?

b. go to bed before your favorite
   TV program is over?

Note to teacher: Check to see that all the students have added a mouth
to the two sample exercises. Then read each activity below as the students
complete the inventory.

How do you feel when you

1. go to school?

4. have music?

2. count money?

5. have math problems
   that are easy?

3. add numbers?

6. subtract numbers?

Fig. 4.2 Example items from an attitude toward mathematics scale for the primary
level.

Name_____

DIRECTIONS: Please write your name in the upper righthand corner. Each of the statements on this form expresses a feeling which a particular person has toward mathematics. Please read each statement carefully. Decide whether you strongly agree (SA), agree (A), are undecided (U), disagree (D), or strongly disagree (SD) with each statement. Then put a check in the blank which best indicates how closely you agree or disagree with the feeling expressed in each statement as it concerns *YOU*. Please read carefully and answer honestly. The results will not affect your grade.

SA   A   U   D   SD

1. Math is logical.

2. I study math because I feel it to be an obligation.

3. Math should be avoided whenever possible.

4. I am happier in math class than in any other class.

5. Math is a waste of time.

6. There are too many chances to make a mistake in math.

7. I have never liked math, and it is my most dreaded subject.

8. I feel a definite positive reaction to math; it's enjoyable.

9. I never go beyond the assigned problems in math.

10. It is fun to play with numbers.

11. There is little need for math in most jobs, except for science and engineering.

12. I believe that math is the most important of the subjects I have studied.

13. My aim in math is to master the essentials as quickly and painlessly as possible.

14. I would love to teach math.

15. Math puzzles do not interest me at all.

16. I feel that math is vital to my future.

Fig. 4.3 Middle school attitude toward mathematics scale.

the same as the psychological distance from "Agree" to "Undecided" (2 to 3). If one is not comfortable with the assumption of equal intervals, then each item should be analyzed separately.

Observation Checklists

The responses to affective rating scales are often influenced by students' deciding how the teacher wants the items answered and answering in accordance with the teacher's goals rather than in accordance with reality. Observation strategies can avoid this problem and in this way obtain a more accurate assessment of typical student performance. However, observational data can be extremely unreliable unless they are gathered in a systematic way. A checklist should be used to focus attention on the specific behaviors to be observed. Usually the observer merely checks whether a particular behavior occurred but sometimes a value judgment about the behavior is also required. It is important to note that observers can very reliably check whether a behavior occurred. This precision breaks down though when the observer must make inferences about the behavior or the reasons why the student behaved in such a way. For example, it would be easy to determine that a student did not participate in a group discussion. It would be much harder to decide whether the reason for nonparticipation was because of uneasiness in that particular group or because the assigned material had not been read.

Use with individuals and groups of students. Checklists can be aggregated across students to provide a description of typical performance for a group of students. However, the usual use is to provide data about a particular student to supplement the information on the cognitive objectives. In this sense, checklists fit well with instructional programming for the individual student.

Frequently the observation schemes require the observer to observe a particular student at regular time intervals to provide a chronological record of behavior. For example, an observer might study the ratio of on-task to off-task behaviors by checking whether the student is on-task at fifteen second intervals. Then a ratio can be computed to provide the numerical value for comparison with a criterion or with other students.

The observation checklist presented in Figure 4.4 illustrates the kind of instrument that requires very few inferences on the part of the observer. Hence, the agreement among several observers should be high. The resulting data would provide an accurate description of the activities of an individual student.

Directions: At fifteen second intervals record the behavior(s) in which the target student is engaged.

The student is:

A. Looking at

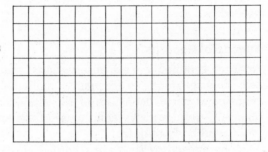

   1. the teacher
   2. a classmate
   3. a group of classmates
   4. a book
   5. a paper
   6. the window,
      ceiling or floor
   7. other

B. Doing

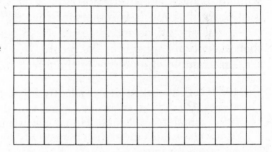

   1. listening
   2. speaking to teacher
   3. speaking to classmate
   4. speaking to a group
   5. reading
   6. writing
   7. computing
   8. other

C. With

   1. no one
   2. the teacher
   3. another student
   4. several students

Fig. 4.4 Observation checklist for student use of free time.

Interpretation of results. The main problem with such observational records is how to synthesize the data and interpret the results. Torgerson (1947, p. 180) clearly indicated that these checklists are difficult to interpret, and they reveal symptoms rather than causes. However, the data accurately describe the typical performance of the student. When the typical performance is task-oriented, productive, and cooperative, the teachers can make judgments about the student. Recording such data will make it easier to explain the typical behavior to parents and administrators. Trying to remember these behaviors is virtually impossible. One usually remembers the exceptions rather than the typical behaviors of students. It is also true that belated descriptions of an event rarely bear any resemblance to what actually took place. Thus it is best to schedule reliable observation at regular intervals. Only then will an adequate data base be available when needed.

Anecdotal Records

Another commonly used observational method is the anecdotal record. This technique is frequently maligned because the record often contains atypical behaviors of the student rather than usual performance. Careful and systematic use of the anecdotal records can result in a useful body of data.

The anecdotes that are recorded should be short descriptions of student behaviors. Interpretations of the behaviors should be done cautiously if at all. It is important that if this method is used the observations should be made regularly so that typical behavior rather than exceptions appear on the record.

An example of an entry in the affective domain might be:

10/21   Bill worked independently for forty minutes on a set of math games. He did the exercises several times until he was able to successfully complete each one. He stayed with the task longer than most of his classmates did. After the activity he said, "I really like to work on number games."

The data from anecdotal records could be linked to the instructional objectives, but they usually are not. The data would most often provide information when programming instruction for the individual student at the point where the teachers decide on the appropriate specific objectives for the individual students.

Unobtrusive Measures

Observation schemes provide good measures of typical student performance as long as the observation is conducted in a natural setting. When the observer intrudes too much, an artificial, experimental atmosphere can be created which presents an inhibiting factor. The students may not behave as they would if an observer were not present. A way around this problem has been presented by Webb, et al. (1968). They suggest that useful data can be gathered unobtrusively without the students' knowing it. For example, a measure of independent reading can be taken from library records or class sign-out

Unobtrusive measures such as the extent to which students use manipulatives in a science lab are indicators of student attitude.

sheets. The number and kind of books selected by each student is available from the normally imposed classroom procedures. The students are not aware of the use that the teachers will make of the data so they will have no reason to introduce bias into the data.

Another example of unobtrusive measures would be when the teacher sets out supplementary geometric figures to reinforce some mathematics concepts. Instruction might be judged to be motivating when those figures become worn and dirty. If the objects continue to look new, then the students are not using them. This kind of information provides a group record rather than an individual record but is free from the influence of teacher expectations.

Unobtrusive measures of student behavior provide a check on the validity of the rating scales and observational data. If the unobtrusive indicators all suggested negative outcomes and the paper-and-pencil scales suggested positive outcomes, one would question the validity of the paper-and-pencil scales first because these are more likely to be susceptible to faking in the preferred direction. Of course, it is possible that there is some unrecognized bias in the unobtrusive data, but this would be less likely than invalid responses to rating scales.

EXAMPLE OF AFFECTIVE EVALUATION USING INDIVIDUALLY GUIDED MOTIVATION (IGM)

Individually guided motivation (Klausmeier, et al. 1973) is a system designed to enable teachers to encourage children to learn well and to like school. The system has many facets, but one of the primary methods of application is through conferences. Small-group conferences with say, three or so students, can be used to help the students become increasingly self-directed. Conferences are usually about 20 minutes in length, and it is recommended that they be held once a week.

The detailed procedures for conducting small-group conferences will not be discussed here, but one characteristic of such conferences is that evaluation of student response and behavior must occur throughout the conference. The students' progress and the procedures of applying motivational principles are assessed.

Table 4.1 contains a listing of objectives for a small-group conference and an assessment checklist covering three conferences. Note that the list is comprehensive and covers four major groupings of affective objectives. There is a checklist for each student. The teacher and the student can fill out the checklist during the conference and at the end of the conference. Completing the checklist is assessment. The two categories, "needs improvements" and "satisfactory," are straightforward, and immediate judgments can be made. Thus, evaluation is a joint activity between teacher and student.

The evaluation need not be limited to on-the-spot evaluation during the conference. In an IGE school the teachers of an I & R Unit can meet to discuss the behavior of the students and the data from the conferences. Basically, there are two foci of the evaluation: (1) the progress of students in meeting the affective objectives, and (2) the teachers' ability to conduct conferences.

With regard to student progress, evaluation should not be limited to considering conference responses. It should be noted whether the student is working toward the affective objectives between conferences as well. The evaluation should consider change in specific student behaviors and not be limited to improvement in overall behavior.

With respect to evaluating a teacher's skill in conducting conferences there are two commonly used approaches; have teachers rate themselves, and have them rate each other. A list of guidelines formed into a checklist is presented in Table 4.2. This list can be used for self-evaluation or for evaluating others. It covers a series of conferences and can therefore be used across conferences for comparison. Ratings should be done at regular intervals and the results discussed among the teachers. This approach to evaluation is somewhat informal, but it is based on data related to specific procedures.

Another approach to evaluating skill in conducting a conference is to audiotape or videotape the conference and to play it back at a staff meeting. This approach has obvious advantages over using checklist data only since the actual behaviors of teachers and students can be heard and/or seen firsthand. Using this approach is, of course, dependent upon the availability of the equipment and support technicians.

MEASURING PSYCHOMOTOR VARIABLES

Most classroom teachers do very little assessment in the psychomotor domain although they are aware of its influence on cognitive and affective performance. Motor development in younger children, their physical maturity, imposes practical limits on the effectiveness of certain teaching. For example, the time to introduce cursive handwriting is largely determined by the hand coordination of the students.

Psychomotor Objectives

When programming instruction for the individual student, objectives in the psychomotor domain are set for the student, as are objectives in the cognitive and affective domains. Harrow (1972) has developed a taxonomy of objectives in the psychomotor domain. The taxonomy contains six major classification levels with subcategories within each classification level. The six major classification levels are as follows:

1. Reflex movements
2. Basic-fundamental movements
3. Perceptual abilities
4. Physical abilities
5. Skilled movements
6. Nondiscursive communications

Table 4.1 Objectives for Small-group Conferences Dealing with Self-directedness and Prosocial Behavior with Assessment Checklist

Name of Pupil _____

Directions: Rate the child on each of the behaviors listed below.	Date:		Date:		Date:	
	Needs improvement	Satisfactory	Needs improvement	Satisfactory	Needs improvement	Satisfactory
A. Behaviors related to self-directedness outside the small-group conferences:						
1. The child works toward goals and on school tasks with minimum teacher assistance.						
2. The child continues working toward goals and on school tasks when the teacher is not present.						
3. The child persists until tasks are accomplished.						
4. The child raises questions about how to bring about improvements in school and/or home or neighborhood conditions.						
5. The child plans own use of free time to carry out worthwhile activities.						

6. The child tries to find ways to improve own conditions and also the conditions of others.									
B. Behaviors related to care of property:									
1. The child takes good care of own clothing, books, and other belongings.									
2. The child takes good care of other people's clothing, books, and other belongings.									
3. The child takes good care of the school's supplies, materials, and equipment.									
4. The child has materials ready when needed.									
5. The child stores materials where they belong.									
6. The child reports any damage done to school property or other people's belongings.									
C. Behaviors related to conduct involving relations with people:									
1. The child gets to class and other activities on time.									
2. The child pays attention to suggestions from teachers, aides, or classmates.									
3. The child does share of a group activity.									

Table 4.1 (cont.)

Directions: Rate the child on each of the behaviors listed below.	Date:		Date:		Date:	
	Needs improvement	Satisfactory	Needs improvement	Satisfactory	Needs improvement	Satisfactory
4. The child goes to and from activities without disturbing others.						
5. The child helps others and shares with classmates.						
6. The child responds to others courteously and honestly.						
7. The child defends own values, position, and property rather than conforming blindly to the group's values.						
D. Behaviors related to self-directedness during the small-group conferences:						
1. The child states own ideas concisely.						
2. The child pays attention and listens to others.						
3. The child raises questions on points that need clarification.						

4. The child gives reasons for own behaviors.							
5. The child states the effects of possible future actions on the child and on others.							
6. The child sets goals related to self-directedness or prosocial behavior.							
7. The child discusses how to attain goals.							
8. The child reports on and answers questions about progress toward goal attainment.							
9. The child states conditions in school or at home that may have prevented goal attainment.							
10. The child gives suggestions and praise to others.							

Table 4.2 Guidelines for Conducting Small-group Conferences with Self-Assessment Checklist

Name _____

Conference Procedures	Date:		Date:		Date:	
	Needs improvement	Satisfactory	Needs improvement	Satisfactory	Needs improvement	Satisfactory
A. Focusing attention on a problem area:						
1. Greet the group pleasantly.						
2. Call attention to the problem area.						
3. Accept statements that children make, even if you do not agree.						
4. Have the children state the problem in their own words.						
5. Give your undivided attention to the group.						
B. Discussing possible solutions to problems:						
1. Use "why" questions to help the children understand why their problems exist.						
2. Use "what happens when" questions to help the children explore the consequences of various behaviors on themselves and others.						

3. Discuss ideal ways of behaving using "real-life" or symbolic models as examples of desired behaviors.

4. Encourage and reinforce contributions to the discussion, especially contributions by children who seldom take part.

C. Goal setting:

1. Assist each child in setting a realistic goal that will solve the individual child's problem.

2. Discuss ways in which children can remember and work toward their goals.

3. Reinforce participation in goal setting.

4. Tell the children when and where the next conference will be.

Additional Procedures for Later Conferences

D. Assessing goal attainment:

1. Comment on and reinforce children's goal-directed behavior you have observed between conferences.

2. Encourage each child to report on progress toward the goal.

3. Praise the child for progress toward the goal.

Table 4.2 (cont.)

	Date:		Date:		Date:	
	Needs improvement	Satisfactory	Needs improvement	Satisfactory	Needs improvement	Satisfactory
Additional Procedures for Later Conferences						
4. Encourage children to be mutually supportive of each other's progress.						
E. Setting new goals:						
1. Discuss with the group whether to continue work in the same problem area or to move to another area.						
2. If the group decides to continue working in the same problem area, repeat the steps in Section C of this table; if the group decides to move to a *new* problem area, repeat the steps in Sections A, B, and C of this table.						

This taxonomy is in a sense hierarchical in that it goes from the least sophisticated to the most sophisticated types of movements with respect to learner concentration. Reflex movements are involuntary in nature. They are functional at birth and develop through the maturation of the individual.

On the other end of the taxonomy, nondiscursive communication includes behaviors that are both innate and learned. However, the innate behaviors are combinations of reflexes, and as communications represent types of emotional expression. The learned behaviors are those composed of movements performed for the purpose of conveying a message. Note that the higher levels of this taxonomy contain major affective and cognitive components.

Developing taxonomies in the psychomotor domain has not received the attention given taxonomies in the cognitive and affective domains. Perhaps the reason for this is that a psychomotor taxonomy is not as needed by the elementary school teacher. Certainly it is not needed to the extent that cognitive and affective taxonomies are needed. The terms we use to denote physical behaviors are much more precise than terms such as "understand" or "appreciate" traditionally associated with the cognitive and affective domains. The emphasis upon instructional and affective objectives has been in part due to an attempt to identify less vague and more observable behaviors. Behaviors in the psychomotor domain have been highly specific and observable.

Outcomes in psychomotor objectives. The measurement of psychomotor variables is more direct than measurement of cognitive or affective variables. Usually the assessment is done by skilled observers, or the operational definition of the outcome is inherent in the task. Skills such as gymnastics or penmanship would require judgments by observers but other variables such as running or response latency might be measured by a stopwatch. The important consideration is still that the measurement is done validly. There must be agreement that the score does in fact represent what is being measured and that the scores are reliable.

Building Psychomotor Instruments

There are many kinds of apparatus for psychomotor assessment. There are timers, dynabalometers, and dynamometers just to name a few. These are calibrated instruments which are much more precise than human judgments or paper-and-pencil devices. However, these instruments do not exist for most variables so we must again rely on observation checklists and rating scales.

The steps to be followed in building psychomotor measures are similar to those developed earlier.

1. Define the attribute to be measured. Use specific behavioral descriptors of the desired student performance.

2. Develop a list of statements covering all important aspects of the performance.

3. Determine the graduations of performance on the continuum that will be used for assigning the ratings.

4. Give clear, precise directions on how to record responses.

Examples of Psychomotor Measures

The simplest type of checklist merely requires a yes-no judgment on the part of the observer. The checklist in Figure 4.5 is representative of this kind of instrument (Williams 1974). Since a judgment is required, observers should be trained and their consistency should be established.

The example of Figure 4.5 deals with running and either the student does or does not exhibit the behavior. The teacher, most likely the physical education teacher, could have several students going through the running exercise simultaneously. However, the measurement is on individual students. As individuals do or do not demonstrate the behavior, appropriate instruction can be provided. This is in keeping with the concept of instructional programming for the individual student.

Not all psychomotor assessment is limited to the physical education period. Assessment can include activities that take place in the day-to-day instructional setting. A checklist appropriate for such assessment appears in Figure 4.6.

The checklist of Figure 4.6 requires considerable interpretation on the part of the observer. The list consists of only ten items taken from the Rhode Island Pupil Identification Scale (Novack, et al. 1972). Notice that words like "difficulty" require more inferences about the behavior than were required of the behaviors in Figure 4.5. Similarly, although the five-point scale provides a measure of degree, it also requires the observer to make additional judgments. Again, observers should have some training so that there is consistency to their ratings. A practice session in which all observers rate the same student would allow a discussion to take place which would better define the points on the scale. In Individually Guided Education it is expected that the unit leader of an I & R Unit would coordinate any practice or training sessions.

Running

Name _____ Age _____ Sex _____

1. Trunk inclined slightly forward.

   Yes _____   No _____

2. Arms and legs used in operation.

   Yes _____   No _____

3. Arms swing freely; close to the body (large arc in sagittal plane).

   Yes _____   No _____

4. Arms bent (slightly) at elbows.

   Yes _____   No _____

5. Head erect; facing forward.

   Yes _____   No _____

6. Support foot hits floor, heel first. The placement of the foot may become approximately flat as speed increases and is very close to body.

   Yes _____   No _____

7. Body stays close to ground (little elevation).

   Yes _____   No _____

8. Extension and flexion evident in both limbs. (Knee flexed as it swings through; support leg extends as it pushes off.)

   Yes _____   No _____

Fig. 4.5 Behavioral checklist for psychomotor measurement.

Teachers might find it useful to develop a scale of their own or use an available scale like the Rhode Island scale. This type of scale is helpful in identifying chronic psychomotor problems or lack of expected development. When programming instruction for the individual student, information from psychomotor evaluation is helpful at the step where specific objectives are formulated for the individual student. The systematic use of an instrument assures a better data base and more uniform interpretation of the data. That is, when all of the teachers have access to all of the data on a particular student, there is more agreement about the appropriateness of the resultant objectives.

Psychomotor Skills

Name _____ Age _____ Sex _____

1. Has difficulty cutting.
   ☐ never ☐ rarely ☐ occasionally ☐ frequently ☐ always

2. Has difficulty pasting.
   ☐ never ☐ rarely ☐ occasionally ☐ frequently ☐ always

3. Bumps into objects.
   ☐ never ☐ rarely ☐ occasionally ☐ frequently ☐ always

4. Trips over self.
   ☐ never ☐ rarely ☐ occasionally ☐ frequently ☐ always

5. Has difficulty catching a ball.
   ☐ never ☐ rarely ☐ occasionally ☐ frequently ☐ always

6. Has difficulty jumping rope.
   ☐ never ☐ rarely ☐ occasionally ☐ frequently ☐ always

7. Has difficulty tying shoes.
   ☐ never ☐ rarely ☐ occasionally ☐ frequently ☐ always

8. Has difficulty buttoning buttons.
   ☐ never ☐ rarely ☐ occasionally ☐ frequently ☐ always

9. Has difficulty sitting still.
   ☐ never ☐ rarely ☐ occasionally ☐ frequently ☐ always

10. Has difficulty standing still.
    ☐ never ☐ rarely ☐ occasionally ☐ frequently ☐ always

Fig. 4.6 Items from the Rhode Island Pupil Identification Scale.

A final example, in Figure 4.7, comes from one part of the Williams Gross Motor Coordination Test Battery (1974). Normative data are provided by this instrument since, unlike the instruments of the previous example, criterion-referenced measurement would clearly be arbitrary and inappropriate for these kinds of data.

The detail in the scale is necessary so that all observers follow the same rules for judging performance. Such precision of definition ensures the validity of the measurements. This precision enables people to really know then what each score means. This scale was included

I. Balance

A. Static Balance—Eyes Closed

The child is first asked to stand on one foot (the preferred foot) with hands on hips, then asked to close the eyes and to try to balance for as long as possible. The child is considered to be "out of balance": (a) if hands are removed from hips; (b) if the nonsupport foot touches the ground; (c) if there is excessive movement of the body and/or support foot. The source for a single trial is the number of seconds (to the nearest tenth) that the child remains in a controlled balance position. The performance measure is the average of four consecutive trials. NOTE: if the child remains in balance continuously for 60 seconds on any given trial, that trial is automatically terminated.

B. Balance Beam Walk—Time and Number of Falls

The child is asked to walk (forward) the length of a two-inch balance beam in a heel-to-toe fashion. The heel of one foot must be placed on the beam in such a way that it touches or comes in contact with the toe of the other foot. The child who steps or falls off the balance beam is instructed to step back onto the beam at the point at which the child stepped off and to continue walking (as before) to the end of the beam. Each step off the beam (with either one or both feet) is counted as one "fall." Two scores are recorded for each trial: (a) the total number of falls and (b) the time (to the nearest tenth of a second) required to complete the balance beam walk. Four trials are given. The measure of the child's performance is the average of four trials.

C. Balance Beam Kneel—Time and Number of Falls

The child is asked to walk (forward) to the center of a standard two-inch balance beam. (An "X" or tape mark is used to indicate the center of the beam.) On reaching the center, the child is to kneel down touching one knee (either right or left) to the beam and then to arise from that position and walk to the end of the beam. Falls are measured and scores recorded as for the balance beam walk. Four trials are given. The measure of the child's performance is the average of the four trials.

Fig. 4.7 Item from the Williams Gross Motor Coordination Test Battery.

---

because it serves as a model for the kind of behavioral definition that could be used in many other scales. Defining outcomes in this way avoids the value-laden inferences required of some rating scales. Data from a scale like this are much less apt to be over- or underinterpreted because everyone is clear about what the numbers represent.

The discussion of the instruments for measuring psychomotor performance and the evaluation of the data have been presented in the context of programming instruction for the individual student. Data are collected on individual students and used for setting realistic objectives and developing appropriate tasks for individual students. Psychomotor considerations are not limited to the physical education period. Especially with younger children, appropriate instructional objectives are in part determined by psychomotor considerations. For example, the criterion of acceptable performance of an objective dealing with clarity of penmanship should be influenced by the level of hand coordination of the student.

As students engage in physical exercises, each is being measured on individual performance.

SUMMARY

Data from affective and psychomotor measures are used in evaluation when programming instruction for the individual student. The data are relevant to setting realistic instructional objectives for the student, and developing appropriate instructional programs.

Assessment in the affective domain is conducted in a variety of ways, many of which were discussed and illustrated in this chapter. The teacher uses a combination of data in affective evaluation. The very nature of affective data makes them more subjective than data in the cognitive and psychomotor domains. This does not make affective data any less relevant to decisions about instructional programming, however.

Evaluation of psychomotor performance can take place both within the physical education period and in the usual instructional setting. Instruments appropriate for assessment in both settings were presented in this chapter. The behaviors in the psychomotor domain are to a large extent well defined and observable. Nevertheless, judgments are involved about the psychomotor development of the child in and of itself, as well as the relevance of psychomotor performance to the child's cognitive and affective performance.

DISCUSSION TOPICS

1. In what ways do cognitive, affective, and psychomotor objectives contain aspects of the other domains?
2. What are two of the disadvantages that are common to both rating scales and observation checklists?
3. Are anecdotal records or unobtrusive measures likely to be misused by teachers? Why?
4. What kinds of psychomotor information would teachers like to have on children ages eight to ten?

REFERENCES

Harrow, A. J. 1972. *A taxonomy of the psychomotor domain.* New York: McKay.

Hering, J. 1973. Attitude toward mathematics scale. University of Toledo (mimeo).

Kish, J. 1973. *Project SMILE evaluation.* University of Toledo.

Klausmeier, H. J., D. A. Frayer, and M. R. Quilling 1973. *Individually guided motivation,* Madison, Wisc.: Wisconsin Research and Development Center for Cognitive Learning.

Krathwohl, D. R., *et al.* 1964. *Taxonomy of educational objectives: Handbook II, Affective Domain,* New York: McKay.

Novack, H. S., E. Bonaventura, and P. F. Merenda 1972. Rhode Island Pupil Identification Scale.

Torgerson, T. L. 1947. *Studying children, diagnostic and remedial procedures in teaching,* New York: Dryden.

Webb, E. J., D. T. Campbell, R. D. Schwartz, and L. Sechrest 1966. *Unobtrusive measures: nonreactive research in the social sciences.* Chicago: Rand McNally.

Williams, H. G. 1974a. Motor characteristics of perceptual-motor development: process descriptions and evaluations. University of Toledo (mimeo).

———— 1974b. Gross Motor Coordination Test Battery. University of Toledo (mimeo).

5
Factors That Affect Test Scores

Objectives

After reading this chapter, the reader will be able:

- To identify student characteristics that influence test performance.
- To identify aspects of test administration that influence test performance.
- To explain ways to minimize the contaminating effects of student and administrative characteristics.
- To relate influences on test scores to the various item formats.

An expanding body of literature exists today dealing with the various factors which influence test scores other than the competence level of the student. These contaminating factors cause people with the same level of competence to score differently on a test. With a criterion-referenced test it is quite posible that the gain or loss due to these extraneous factors would be enough to put some students above the criterion and other students, with the same true level of competence, below the criterion. Hence, these influences on test scores should be recognized and kept to a minimum whenever possible.

It is important to note that most of the research in this area has been done with students in high school or college. The results should be generalized to other age groups with great caution. Many classroom teachers believe, however, that the results found with older students are even more pronounced with younger children. These opinions still need to be empirically investigated though.

STUDENT CHARACTERISTICS

There are student characteristics, such as test-taking habits and personality traits, that are associated with differential performance on tests. This causes a situation in which the effects of these traits or variables cannot be separated from the test performance. We say that these effects are confounded with test performance. If the influence of these confounding variables can be controlled or at least recognized, the teacher is in a better position to make decisions on test scores. It is our intention to share some of these influences and make suggestions about how they might be minimized. These kinds of influences exist regardless of the form of instructional programming, and they merit consideration when programming instruction for the individual student.

Guessing

Whenever the student selects the correct response from a list of options (as in true-false, multiple-choice, or matching items) there is a certain specifiable probability that the test taker could merely guess the right answer. This probability is $p = 1/K$, where K is the number of options. For example, the probability of guessing correctly on a true-false item is 1/2, on a four-option multiple-choice item it is 1/4. Note that this probability of guessing the correct response is for specific items.

The number of items on a test that one could be expected to guess correctly equals $n \times p$, i.e., the number of items on the test multiplied by the probability of guessing an item correctly. So, for a

100-item true-false test, a student could be expected to guess correctly on fifty items ($100 \times 1/2 = 50$). Similarly, twenty-five items could be guessed correctly on a 100-item, four-option, multiple-choice test.

Since not all guessers will get exactly $n \times p$ items correct, there will be a distribution of chance scores. Refer to Chapter 2 if you need to refresh your statistical memory. The shape of this distribution will be similar to the normal curve with a mean of $n \times p$ and a standard deviation of $\sqrt{n \times p \times q}$ where $q = 1 - p$. Figure 5.1 illustrates the distribution of chance scores for a 100-item multiple-choice test with four options per item. Notice that a score of 30 could clearly be achieved by someone who merely guessed at every item.

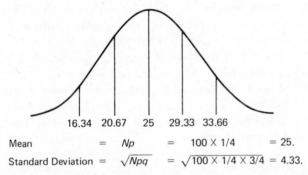

	16.34	20.67	25	29.33	33.66

Mean $\quad\quad\quad\quad = \quad Np \quad = \quad 100 \times 1/4 \quad = 25.$

Standard Deviation $= \quad \sqrt{Npq} \quad = \sqrt{100 \times 1/4 \times 3/4} = 4.33.$

Fig. 5.1 Distribution of chance scores on a 100-item, four-option, multiple-choice test.

One could use a "Correction for Chance Formula" to bring the guesser's score back to zero. Such a formula is

$$\text{Score} = \#\text{ right} - \frac{\#\text{ wrong}}{\#\text{ options} - 1}.$$

This formula adjusts the score by the amount an examinee could have been expected to guess correctly.

For example, say that Jill takes a true-false test of 40 items. If she really knows the answer to only 10 of those items and guesses on the remaining 30 items, we could expect that her score will be 10 plus 15 (half of the 30 items she guessed on) or 25 points. Her exact score may differ from 25 if she doesn't guess right exactly half of the time. If she got 25 items right, she must have gotten 15 items wrong. Applying the formula yields:

$$\text{Score} = 25 - \frac{15}{2 - 1} = 10.$$

The formula then merely corrects the score by the amount that a student could be expected to guess correctly. Changes in the formula which actually penalize the guesser are occassionally used but rarely in a classroom situation.

It is more important that the teachers know the expected chance score, the guesser's score, than it is to use some complicated correction formula. Probably one should not try to interpret scores that are fewer than two standard deviations above a chance score. In terms of the example in Figure 5.1, this would mean that only scores above 34 can be reasonably thought to be different from a guesser's score.

For criterion-referenced tests it is important that the criterion level of minimal acceptable performance be well above the expected chance score. This will almost always be the case. For the data in Figure 5.1, this would mean that the criterion level should be set above 34. On a 100-item test, the criterion level would surely be above this point. However, note that students might capitalize on chance when there is a small number of items on a test. They could guess enough items correctly to exceed the criterion level on the total test. Children will often perform at the chance level on a pretest covering material they know little or nothing about. This result should be expected and neither the teacher nor the students should be anxious about such low test scores.

Positional Preference

Another student response characteristic is to select an answer based on the position of the response rather than the content of the response. The rule "when in doubt, pick option c" is an example that works for multiple-choice tests built by naive test constructors. As for distractors, the first one comes easy, the second one is harder to think of. A third distractor is hard to think of, so position "c" is taken by the correct answer. Finally, the "d" position is filled by a weak distractor. When tests are built in such a fashion the test-wise student notices a preponderance of correct answers in the "c" position. Hence, when the student is unsure, option "c" is selected. Unfortunately, a student who selects "c" for every item does well on this kind of a test. Similar problems occur when the test builder makes too many items true or too many items false on a true-false test.

It is easy to guard against positional preference influence by merely making sure that the correct answers appear in a random sequence. Perhaps an easier technique is to order the options numerically (such as dates in a history item) or alphabetically depending on the kind of answer sought. This strategy minimizes the possibility for a pattern of correct responses which the test-wise student could identify.

Changing Answers

Much folklore exists about the wisdom of changing answers on multiple-choice tests. Are first impressions correct or is a second reading more accurate? In a study of college students, Reiling and Taylor (1972) found that changing answers clearly resulted in improved test scores. Perhaps the reason why some students believe the opposite is because answers changed from right to wrong tend to be remembered longer than answers changed from wrong to right.

Perhaps teachers should tell students to answer the questions carefully and then to check over the answers if there is enough time. Upon a second reading, some answers may appear wrong. If that is the case, then change the answer. The only caution should be that the student should not read into the questions more information than is provided.

Bluffing

Student characteristics influencing responses to essay tests also give rise to a set of problems. A test-wise student is probably at an even greater advantage with this kind of test as compared to objective-type tests. A study by Bracht and Hopkins (1968) with high school students has shown that scores on essay tests are definitely related to the length of the response. High scores are given to students who write a great deal, regardless of what they say.

The way to minimize such a contaminant is to give very specific directions and identify specific criteria for the response. Appropriate length of the response can be specified. Preparing a model answer before scoring the tests does a great deal to make sure that the scorer pays heed to question related responses instead of just to responses. Otherwise, one rewards general verbal ability rather than mastery of the objectives covered by the test.

Penmanship, Spelling, Etc.

Essay scores have also been shown to be related to the clarity of penmanship of the student. The easier it is to read the answer, the better the score that is given (Chase 1968, Marshall and Powers 1969). Unfortunately, the quality of penmanship is rarely linked with the quality of the response. Hence, test scorers should make sure that they are not influenced by the student's penmanship, when in fact penmanship is not being evaluated.

Perhaps the simplest way to guard against such irrelevant factors is again to use a model answer. This strategy focuses the scorer's attention. Scores are then more concerned with the content of the response than with its appearance.

Other similar influences are the use of correct spelling, proper English, and appropriate punctuation. Essay grades could possibly be more a function of these elements than a function of the content of the response. It is important that these be a part of the grade only if they are a part of the criteria of the objectives covered by the test. If so, both the students and the teachers should know what proportion of the grade is due to these factors.

Essay questions in tests are used sparingly, especially with younger children such as those of primary level. However, the comments relative to these factors apply when teachers are evaluating work samples. They should be influenced by factors such as penmanship only to the extent that they are part of the criteria of the objectives being covered.

Anxiety

The factors discussed above are basically mechanical factors with respect to responding to items. There are personality characteristics that are related to a student's test score too. Test anxiety is a commonly mentioned factor affecting test scores regardless of the kind of items on the test. Numerous research studies (Chambers, *et al.* 1972) have shown that there is a low, negative correlation between test anxiety and test performance. That is, the students with the higher levels of test anxiety tend to score lower on the cognitive test. The relationship is not a strong one although it consistently appears in the research literature.

Note that this relationship is strictly correlational, and correlations by themselves do *not* imply cause and effect. Students often say that they did poorly *because* of a high level of anxiety. Teachers often say that the students were anxious *because* they were not prepared to take the test. Or, students who do poorly on the first items of the test, not knowing any of the answers, become anxious. Upon completing the test and recognizing they know little, they experience high anxiety. Any or none of these explanations could be correct. The correlation does not indicate which explanation is correct; it merely indicates the inverse relation between the two variables. Higher test scores are associated with lower test anxiety but no cause-and-effect explanation can be made.

Teachers can help to minimize the effects of this phenomenon by trying to make testing situations as nonanxiety-producing as possible. The tests should not be built up out of proportion. In fact, Jensen and Schmitt (1970) have shown that the test title can induce a response set that changes the students' performance. Similarly, anxiety-producing instructions can result in poorer test performance for some students.

Having test content based directly on instructional objectives, as is the case when programming instruction for the individual student, should tend to be among the least anxiety-producing kinds of testing arrangements. Whether published or teacher-constructed tests are used, labeling tests with the objectives in the instructional sequence will surely be less intimidating than many of the longer published titles for achievement or aptitude tests. In addition, the content validity of the test, that is, the match between what has been recently taught and items on the test, should reduce student anxiety.

Effects on Reliability and Validity

The effects of many of the influences discussed above on test performance are usually quite different depending on whether one is speaking about the reliability or the validity of the test. Most individual characteristics have consistent effects from one testing situation to another. For example, the bold gambler tends to guess on test items whenever the opportunity exists, regardless of the kind of test. Obviously this consistency of performance is reflected in the reliability of the test. If these characteristics affect the reliability of the tests at all, the tendency is for them to increase the reliability.

The effect on validity is quite different, however, as one scores for penmanship instead of for content, or as the testing situation intimidates the impressionable student, the meaning of the test score becomes blurred. The test score is less representative of what it is intended to measure, mastery of an objective. The result of such a situation is that the test lacks validity.

There are many student characteristics and test-taking habits that influence test scores. Teachers should be cognizant of these factors so that they might take steps to minimize the confounding effects. As these effects interfere, the validity of the test is weakened. The test cannot measure what it is designed to measure when extraneous variables affect the scores.

These contaminants are individual. They may affect the scores of some but not all of the students in the class. Other, more general, problems can affect all students. These are typically products of the variations in ways that the tests are administered. These factors are usually more easily recognized and hence can be more easily controlled by the teachers.

ADMINISTRATIVE CHARACTERISTICS

The testing situation itself can introduce facilitating or inhibiting factors which influence test scores. Most of these extraneous variables have been well studied so we have a good notion about their effects.

Fortunately, the testing setting is a factor that is directly controlled by the teachers.

Different testing procedures may be dictated by the age level of the students and the content area that is tested. For example, younger children will probably be tested in reading through samples of oral reading and older children will probably be tested in mathematics through work sheets that the teacher constructs or obtains with published curriculum materials. However, the studies on the administrative characteristics of testing can provide useful guidelines for teachers who are responsible for establishing and maintaining the testing component when individualizing instruction for the student.

The Use of Separate Answer Sheets

Many teachers like to use separate answer sheets so that scoring can be done faster or so that the test copies can be reused. There is some concern about the appropriateness of separate answer sheets for younger children.

Research by Ramseyer and Cashen (1971) indicated that above average first and second graders could not handle separate answer sheets even when they were given practice sessions. Recording responses directly on the test paper resulted in significantly fewer errors.

It is generally agreed that by the end of the third grade and certainly by fourth grade students can use separate answer sheets without any appreciable effect on their scores (Cashen and Ramseyer 1969).

The Testing Arrangements

There is also concern about the physical arrangements in the room where the tests are given. In a study with ninth grade students Ingle and DeAmico (1969) found that standardized achievement tests could be given in an auditorium with lap boards and have the results not differ significantly from those of tests given in normal classroom situations.

The person who administers the test can also be a factor. Hopkins *et al.* (1967) found that when the classroom teacher administered the tests, the scores tended to be higher than when someone else administered them.

It would seem then that students can perform well on tests given in almost any physical arrangement as long as control and rapport are established. Moderate variations in the testing situations affect scores negligibly. Perhaps the test administrator is more important than the testing conditions.

The physical arrangements in the rooms of most individualized programs allow a great deal of flexibility for changing the testing

Separate answer sheets should be used with older children only.

setting. Testing could be done in large groups, small groups, or individually. A part of the room could be designated as a testing center or students could work at their desks. Neither arrangement should affect the test scores. It is more important that the teachers direct and monitor the testing situation so that the students are aware of their concern and interest.

The Effect of Practice

Since programming instruction for the individual student involves frequent testing to monitor student progress, the effect on students of repeated testing is particularly relevant. Callenbach (1973) studied the effect of having second grade students practice taking tests. He found that even when the content of the practice tests differed from the content of the criterion tests the second graders performed significantly better when they had been given practice sessions.

Perhaps the important implication of the Callenbach study is that it is not unethical, in fact it helps, to teach students how to take tests. Students may score poorly on a test because they are awestruck or intimidated by the testing situation, not because they have not mastered the content. It is the responsibility of the teachers to make sure that the test is a valid measure of student competence rather than student reaction to the testing situation.

Group Versus Individual Testing

A study by Niedermeyer and Sullivan (1972) has particular meaning for individualized programs. This study compared the effectiveness of individually administered, constructed response tests, an oral reading exercise and group administered multiple-choice tests with first graders. They found that the constructed response and four-option, multiple-choice tests worked well. Three-option, multiple-choice items did not adequately identify the poor readers. Meetings with the participating first grade teachers indicated that the teachers preferred the individually administered, constructed-response tests for the following reasons:

> easier to administer
> takes less time if they refrain from "on the spot" remediation
> eliminates copying
> gives the teacher better knowledge of an individual child's skill level
> makes the child feel good when he receives the individual attention of the teacher (p. 203)

The reasons cited above are important enough to provide reasons for using individualized testing programs at the primary levels. The choice of item formats seemed to cause a difference in how teachers thought the students felt about the tests. However, it is quite possible that going over the responses to a multiple-choice test with individual students might promote some of these same kinds of desirable results. Apparently, an important consideration is that the testing program promotes a one-to-one relationship between the teacher and the student. Certainly instructional programming for the individual student maximizes the possibility of this happening.

The Possibility of Retesting

When programming instruction for the individual student, there is opportunity for relearning and enrichment when a student has not met the criteria for the instructional objectives. How do students react to a test when they know that they will have the opportunity to retake a criterion test if they are not successful the first time? One might speculate that the students would be less anxious about this kind of test and would use the test situation as more of a learning experience than would students with a traditional "end-of-the-line" type of test. Although this speculation seems logical, research on this factor is needed.

TESTING IN INDIVIDUALIZED PROGRAMS

There are some aspects of instructional programming for the individual student that imply particular measurement needs that do not appear very frequently in traditional programs. Most of these considerations are due to the necessity of having a record of student performance on each of the instructional objectives. Such a complete monitoring of student progress will naturally result in a large number of assessments. A lot of testing places demands upon the instructional staff since these tests should be stimulating enough to maintain student interest and rapport and they should be learning experiences for the student while gathering useful information for making decisions about student learning. To be sure, testing is not the only form of assessment used, but it is an important form. Thus it is important to look at some characteristics of the test which affect the testing situation.

Pretests and Posttests

There is some question about whether the pretest and the posttest over an objective or a set of objectives should be identical. If these tests are identical, then changes in test scores are directly comparable. If, for example, a student gets 10 percent of the items correct on the pretest and 90 percent of the items correct when the same test is given as a posttest, then the gain is easily determined. Such gain scores (posttest score minus pretest score) are intuitively very pleasing but they are statistically disappointing. Nunnally (1967) pointed out that even when the pretest and posttest are reliable, the gain score is notoriously unreliable.

Giving identical pretests and posttests has another disadvantage as indicated by Campbell and Stanley (1966). Some gain in the scores might be merely due to students' remembering some of the items. Practice on these items on the pretest could result in increased posttest scores, especially if the time interval between the two testings is short. Perhaps using parallel forms instead of the exact same items would eliminate this disadvantage. Such a strategy would also provide a wider sampling of the domain of all possible items which would strengthen any inferences about student performance on the whole domain.

A stronger argument against identical pretests and posttests is that they often are designed to serve two very different purposes. In Chapter 2 we warned that tests which are valid for one purpose may not be valid for another purpose. Let us see how a test which is valid as a posttest may not be valid as a pretest.

When using objectives-based instruction the posttest serves a major purpose—successful performance on this test indicates mastery of the particular objective. The pretest, however, serves two functions. Successful performance on the pretest may also indicate mastery of the objective but unsuccessful pretest scores should provide diagnostic information with regard to mastery of necessary prerequisites. Theoretically, differential performance on the pretest should suggest varying instructional strategies. These dual roles are almost contradictory. On the one hand the test should certify terminal mastery of the objective. On the other hand, the test should also be capable of pinpointing areas of specific deficiencies of students who fail to meet the criterion. Decisions about alternative teaching strategies are not facilitated by test results that only show that the student has not mastered the objective.

It seems that what is needed is a pretest that is longer than the corresponding posttest. This is suggested because there may be times when the diagnostic and the certifying items are different. For example, a pretest on long division would include long division items but it might also include multiplication and subtraction items for diagnostic purposes. This dual function of the pretest might also be served by the scoring process for the test. Perhaps in the pretest on long division, only long division items would be included but incorrect answers would be scored in such a way that would isolate the particular student mistakes, that is, multiplication errors, subtraction errors, division procedure errors (diagnostic item sets as discussed in Chapter 3).

How then should teachers construct pretests and posttests for objectives-based programs? Clearly, the pretest should contain an adequate number of items which are congruent with the objective, so that the student has the possibility of satisfying the criterion of the objective on the pretest. The pretest should also contain items on the prerequisite skills and subordinate concepts so that adequate diagnostic information will be available to serve as a basis for decisions about grouping and instruction. Some teachers may decide to separate these two functions into two separate and distinct tests.

The posttest really needs only to contain one set of items, that is, those items which sample the domain of possible items which are determined by the objective. Diagnostic information is not important here unless the student does not attain the objective. In that case, a diagnostic portion could be given as a follow-up to the major part of the test.

Repeated Posttests

Instructional programming for the individual student allows the possibility of some students taking the posttest for an objective or a set of objectives repeatedly until the criterion level is attained. It is unwise to use the same posttest over and over again. Students focus on the specific test items rather than the domain which the items represent. Similarly when only one form of the posttest is used there is always the possibility of students' discussing the posttest items. Since students take the posttests at different times depending on their individual rates of progress, it is quite possible that students who have completed the posttest might share information about the test items with their friends. For both of these reasons it is unwise to regularly use the same posttest again and again.

The problems above can be lessened if teachers prepare or select parallel forms of the posttests for repeated testings. This strategy requires more teacher effort but it solves the problem of using the same items for all students. Since students are not being compared one to another, it is not important that they respond to the same tasks on items. But it is important, however, to make sure that the several tests similarly represent the domain of items and that the criterion level is equivalent across the different forms of the test.

Constructing parallel forms can be facilitated by keeping an adequate file of test items. It is a good practice for teachers to construct or obtain a relatively large number of test items for each of the instructional objectives. Then tests can be generated by selecting from the pool of items whenever a new form of the test is needed. Old items could be refined and additional items could be regularly added to the pool. Frequently items are written on index cards and filed by objective. Then creating parallel tests is quite simple. This procedure is much more satisfactory than starting from nothing whenever a new test is needed.

Another useful approach is to use an item form or item-generating rule. Hively (1974) has shown that such a technique yields equivalent items which represent a common domain. For example, $a + b = c + \underline{\hspace{1cm}}$ could serve as an item-generating rule if teachers defined a,

b, and c as any integers between 1 and 9. Items that might be generated from this rule would be

$$3 + 4 = 6 + \underline{\qquad},$$
$$9 + 9 = 2 + \underline{\qquad},$$
$$1 + 3 = 5 + \underline{\qquad}.$$

Similar defining rules could also be used to avoid negative numbers, to allow certain fractions, or to otherwise change the items so that they would match the objective.

The advantage of this approach is that the item-generating rule assures that equivalent but different items would be used on the different forms of the test. Numbers that satisfy the conditions can be randomly selected so that subtle, systematic biases are avoided.

Take-home and Oral Exams

The necessity of giving frequent tests may spur teachers to use creative testing strategies. Take-home or oral examinations may be substituted for the more traditional forms of testing. Take-home examinations would, of course, not be appropriate for younger children. It is suggested that moves in this direction should be made cautiously for the following reasons.

Take-home examinations have two major problems. First, there is no guarantee that the tests are taken independently. There is no control over the testing situation so there is always the possibility that a variety of human resources might be used, peers, parents, or siblings. Take-home tests could be given for instructional purposes but probably not when the instructional purpose involves evaluation.

Another problem with take-home tests is that students will spend different amounts of time on the tests. More information could be gained from a controlled testing situation with reasonable time limits.

Oral examinations present a different set of problems. The major difficulty with these tests is that the items and the scoring tend to be inconsistent from one instance to another. In fact no two examinations may be alike.

For example, consider an oral test dealing with explaining the water cycle in the student's own words. As the student explains the concept of the water cycle, the teacher has many chances to ask leading questions which would prompt the expected answer. The questions, clues, and nonverbal feedback which the student gets can do much to shape the answer. Teachers would act quite differently in such situations so that the testing setting would not be consistent from one student to another. It is also true that the scoring of oral examinations is quite unreliable. Meeting the criterion is often largely determined by who administers the test rather than what the student says. However, there may be instances when oral examinations are the most appropriate form of measurement. In these cases standard directions and model answers help to reduce the unreliability.

SUMMARY

Clearly, programming instruction for the individual student presents some unique measurement problems. The teacher is actively involved in pretesting and posttesting students on a wide variety of instructional objectives. This responsibility suggests that the staff should be familiar with the complexities of classroom testing. As such, teachers should be aware of the student factors and the test administration factors that might influence test scores. Steps which minimize the confounding effect of these extraneous factors should be an integral part of the testing program.

Student characteristics such as the tendency to guess, to change answers, or to be anxious have been shown to be related to student performance on tests. Teachers need to minimize the effects of these and other confounding factors. Test administration factors such as the use of separate answer sheets, grouping for tests, and the test room itself have been studied as possible influences on test scores. Finally, individualizing instruction itself introduces some factors. Among these are the properties of pretests and posttests, the need for several forms of each test, and the need for a variety of testing methods.

DISCUSSION TOPICS

1. How might teachers give students testlike experiences so that the actual tests are not strange and intimidating?
2. How might teachers use other students to lessen high test anxiety in a student?
3. In what ways do the physical arrangements when individualizing instruction assist the testing situation?
4. What are the advantages and disadvantages of including diagnostic items on a posttest?

REFERENCES

Bracht, G. H., and K. D. Hopkins 1968. Comparative validities of essays and objective tests. Research Paper No. 20, Boulder: Laboratory of Educational Research.

Callenbach, C. 1973. The effects of instruction and practice in content-independent test-taking technique upon the standardized reading test scores of selected second grade students. *Journal of Educational Measurement* 10:25–30.

Campbell, D. T. and J. C. Stanley 1966. *Experimental and quasi-experimental design for research.* Chicago: Rand McNally.

Cashen, V. M. and G. C. Ramseyer 1969. The use of separate answer sheets by primary age children. *Journal of Educational Measurement* 6:155–158.

Chambers, A. C., K. D. Hopkins, and B. R. Hopkins 1972. Anxiety, physiologically and psychologically measured: its effect on mental test performance. *Psychology in the Schools* 9:198–206.

Chase, C. I. 1968. The impact of some obvious variables on essay-test scores. *Journal of Educational Measurement* 5:315–318.

Hively, W. 1974. Introduction to domain-referenced testing. *Educational Technology* 14:5–10.

Hopkins, K. D., D. W. Lefever, and B. R. Hopkins 1967. TV vs. teacher administration of standardized tests: comparability of scores. *Journal of Educational Measurement* 4:35–40.

Ingle, R. B., and G. DeAmico 1969. The effect of physical conditions of the test room on standardized achievement test scores. *Journal of Educational Measurement* 6:237–240.

Jensen, J. A., and J. A. Schmitt 1970. The influence of test title on test response. *Journal of Educational Measurement* 7:241–246.

Marshall, J. C., and J. M. *Powers* 1969. Writing neatness, composition errors and essay grades. *Journal of Educational Measurement* 6:97–101.

Niedermeyer, F. C., and H. J. Sullivan 1972. Differential effects of individual and group testing strategies in an objectives-based instructional program. *Journal of Educational Measurement* 9:199–204.

Nunnally, J. C. 1967. *Psychometric theory.* New York: McGraw-Hill.

Ramseyer, G. C., and V. M. Cashen 1971. The effect of practice sessions on the use of separate answer sheets by first and second graders. *Journal of Educational Measurement* 8:177–181.

Reiling, E., and R. Taylor 1972. A new approach to the problem of changing initial responses to multiple choice questions. *Journal of Educational Measurement,* 9:67–70.

6
Published Tests and Their Uses in Objective-Based Instruction Tests

Objectives

After reading this chapter, the reader will be able:

- To identify criteria that might be used for the selection of published tests.
- To identify several sources of norm-referenced and criterion-referenced published tests.
- To distinguish among test selection at the classroom, district, and state levels.
- To be able to use a published test in an instructional setting.

When programming instruction for the individual student, teachers generally use a combination of teacher-made and published tests. The extent to which published tests are available depends in part on the extent to which published instructional objectives are used. In some cases objectives are available and tests are not, or item pools are available. It then remains for the teacher to form the tests using items from the pool.

In any event, teachers should not become entirely dependent upon published sources for their tests and items. There are two reasons for this. First, dependence on published sources tends to discourage the development of local objectives and their concomitant measures. This situation may tend to inhibit the desired flexibility in

Teachers have many published tests available to them.

developing instructional programs for individual students. Second, the search for published tests which match instructional objectives may be more difficult than constructing the tests themselves.

Nevertheless, there are many curriculum programs, instructional packages, etc., that contain excellent tests and items. It would be unwise for the teacher not to take advantage of these. The purpose of this chapter is to acquaint teachers with some of the kinds of published tests which are available and how they might be used in programming instruction for the individual student.

Published tests are designed to serve a particular purpose. Hence, they may not be appropriate for some uses. Some of these tests may be better used for administrative functions and program evaluation than for teachers' day-to-day decisions about the learning of individual students. Some tests are norm-referenced, some are criterion-referenced, and others seem to be attempts at merging the two. The description of the properties of selected published tests is included in order to provide teachers enough information so that they might select those tests that yield valid and usable data for their purposes.

SELECTION OF APPROPRIATE TESTS

There are several things to be considered in the selection of published tests. Who should select the tests? What should be looked for in the test and test manual? Could the data be gathered through less expensive means? Some of the answers will be dictated by the personnel and resources of the specific school. Other considerations will be more general. These decisions may also vary according to the purpose for which the test will be used.

Technical Considerations

In general, the published test that is selected should be reliable and valid for the selector's purpose. The responsibility for the technical characteristics of the test that is selected belongs to both the test constructor and the test user. The test constructor should provide ample evidence of the logical and empirical support for the test. Publishers should be guided by the *Standards for Educational and Psychological Tests* (1974) which lists the kinds of evidence that are appropriate. These standards use the terms reliability and validity in the same way that they were introduced in Chapter 2.

Just because the test is published does not mean that the test has been shown to be of value. O.K. Buros edits a periodic review of many published tests, the *Mental Measurements Yearbook*. In a recent edition, quoting a statement made ten years earlier he says, "At present, no matter how poor a test may be, if it is nicely packaged and it promises to do all sorts of things which no test can do, the test will find many gullible buyers." (Buros 1961, p. 29). Test selectors would be wise to check the *Mental Measurements Yearbook* to determine whether the tests that they are considering are included in that set of reviews.

The test selector also has responsibility for the technical characteristics. Since *caveat emptor* is the state of affairs, the prudent test selector must know what should be looked for. Perhaps the easiest way to structure the test selector's task is to use a form like the one presented in Figure 6.1. Such a device would allow easy comparison of competing tests.

A close look at the form in Figure 6.1 may help to review some of the technical considerations. The name of the test should be recorded since many tests have very similar names. It also helps communication to make certain that there is no confusion about the form of the test.

The purpose of the test as stated by its developer should be recorded along with the prospective user's purpose. This step is useful to avoid using a test which is designed for screening purposes as a measure of mastery. Similarly, this comparison would clarify the distinction between the administrative and instructional purposes of tests. Presently, too many published tests are being used for purposes for which they were not designed.

The reliability coefficients that are reported for published tests are always specific to the particular technique and sample that were used. A different group of students or a different technique will usually lead to a different value of the reported reliability. In fact, there is a tendency for reliability coefficients of achievement tests to be lower for specific local groups of students than those reported in the manual. For this reason it is recommended that schools run their own reliability checks. The form has space for listing the reported data so that the user can see whether the coefficient based on a sample similar to the local group is adequate. The lack of any reliability data should raise suspicion.

Much space on the form is devoted to validity data. For most tests though, there probably will be some blank lines. It is quite unlikely that an achievement test with content validity as the major concern would provide any criterion-related validity data. For content validity, there are two parts. First, what kind of information is provided? And second, how well do the presented data match the description of the user's program?

If, for example, the objectives which the test measures are different from the objectives of the user's programs, the test is probably not appropriate for the user's purposes.

Name of test _____

Purpose of test: Author _____

Purpose of test: User _____

Reliability

Value	Technique	Sample
_____	_____	_____
_____	_____	_____
_____	_____	_____

Validity

Match with user's program
Poor   Excellent

Content:	List of objectives	____	1 2 3 4 5
	Table of specifications ____	1 2 3 4 5
	Theory	____	1 2 3 4 5
	Other	____	1 2 3 4 5

Criterion-related: Criterion   r   Sample

_____	_____	_____
_____	_____	_____
_____	_____	_____

Construct: Data   Sample   Result

_____	_____	_____
_____	_____	_____
_____	_____	_____

Cost: _____

Norms: (if applicable) _____

Fig. 6.1 Form for rating tests.

Similarly, when evaluating a test for its criterion-related validity, the kinds of application and the results need to be known. The form allows a brief summary of this kind of information. The user can then quickly determine how different tests compare as predictors of the criterion of interest for samples similar to the one intended.

Construct validity data can also be summarized on the form if such data are provided by the test publisher. The nature of the study, the sample, and the results can be listed to provide a sketch of the extent of validation of that particular test.

Costs of the test and related services can be recorded so that, other things being equal, the users will get the most for their money. The cost estimate will also allow teachers to decide whether they could build tests as usable and appropriate as the published tests at a fraction of the cost.

Data on the norm group can be presented for norm-referenced tests. The population which the norm group represents should be defined; and the adequacy of the sampling should be defined and noted.

The information on such a form should allow teachers to discuss more efficiently the relative merits of competing tests. The categories point out some of the criteria by which the tests should be judged. It also helps to have this information present so that the discussion is not dependent on one's recollections of studies and information such as reliability coefficients. The form will not allow enough space for all the documentation that is provided for some tests. In such cases, it would suffice to list those results which bear most directly on factors of the local situation, such as similar age groups or similar instructional settings. In many more cases, the raters will find that the forms will have some blank spaces. There is absolutely no information provided for some tests and for others it is meager. In these cases, adoption of the tests should be done very cautiously, if at all. Only a strong, logical rationale could support selection of a published test that has no visible empirical support.

Less Technical Considerations

There are other considerations which are less technical but are still very important. These practical problems will be assessed in terms of the school or class situation. For example, the tests must be of an appropriate length. Some tests may be so long as to impinge on other important activities in the school day. Then the teachers will have to decide whether the information gained through testing is worth the time it takes.

Another consideration might be the form in which results are reported for competing tests. Some tests will supply summary records of individual performance which can become a part of the record of progress for the student. Other tests yield results which require an additional clerical step in order to put the test results in a form that will fit into the running record of student performance. The ease of test administration and scoring would also be included in this set of test selection considerations.

An example of a nontechnical consideration is whether or not separate answer sheets can be used with the test. If students are old enough, eight years or older, they can usually handle the separate answer sheets. Such answer sheets can greatly facilitate scoring. If they cannot be conveniently used with a specific test, it may be worthwhile considering other tests.

Although these less technical characteristics of tests are not as important as the technical considerations, they are important enough to merit attention. A technically excellent test will never be well accepted by the teachers if it falls short in terms of these less technical considerations.

The discussion of the past several pages has centered on the selection of tests that are not necessarily designed for specific curriculum materials. Many packages of curriculum materials are accompanied by tests specifically designed for the content of the materials; in some cases items are related to instructional objectives. When tests are designed for specific curriculum materials and the materials are being used for instruction, selection of tests or items may not be a great concern. However, matters such as technical considerations are still important. Attaching a test to a set of curriculum materials does not necessarily make it a good test. Comments on tests that accompany curriculum materials are made later in the chapter.

PUBLISHED TESTS FOR DIFFERENT PURPOSES

There are several ways in which a discussion of published tests might be structured. There are differences in the variables measured, whether the scores are norm-referenced or criterion-referenced, or what purposes are served by the tests. This development is organized around the purposes because they will dictate many of these other characteristics.

Administrative Purposes

Most administrative functions of tests have been accomplished by using traditional norm-referenced, standardized, achievement tests. These tests cover large blocks of student learning which are believed to represent a common set of educational goals such as developing reading comprehension, mathematical reasoning, arithmetic computation, and the like. Student performance is compared with that of the norm group. Local or national norms may be used depending upon the nature of the needs of the administrators. A variety of excellent tests is available for this purpose. Most of these tests are reviewed in the Eighth *Mental Measurements Yearbook* (Buros, 1972).

Administrative functions of tests center around two purposes: (1) to make comparisons between the performances of groups, either in direct comparisons of two or more groups or in comparing actual and expected outcomes, and (2) to provide an information base when reporting to parents and the community. An example now follows that illustrates both purposes.

The 111th Street School of Los Angeles, California, is an IGE school that has received funding provided by the Elementary and Secondary Education Act (ESEA), Title I, due to the socioeconomic composition of the community. In a report (Flournoy 1974) about the activities in the program and the achievement of the students,

School personnel use yearly test results in evaluating the instructional program.

the results of standardized tests were reported. Specifically the *Cooperative Primary Test*, *Stanford Achievement Test*, and *Comprehensive Tests of Basic Skills* were used in the 111th Street School.

There were two general objectives which would correspond to educational objectives set at Step 1 in the IPM of IGE. The objectives were set for the 1972–73 school year. These general objectives were applied to reading and arithmetic and were as follows:

1. The percentage of students performing below the second quartile (median) would decrease between pre- and posttesting.

2. The students would demonstrate one month's gain for one month's instruction.

Both objectives require pre- and posttesting for providing empirical results by which the attainment of the objectives can be evaluated. Students were pre- and posttested and the results made available.

The detailed results, which of course were extensive and will not be repeated here, were assembled by the Los Angeles City Unified School District. The results were summarized for the participating schools, divided according to ESEA, Title I Areas. The summary appears in Table 6.1.

The table provides a summary of the student attainment in each school with respect to the two educational objectives. Each school is thus identified as having met the objectives at five, four, or three levels. In addition to this, all the schools that attained the objectives at three levels or more are compared relatively in the table. There might be any number of explanations for the variations in attaining the objectives, but the testing has provided the data base by which decision making can proceed. The 111th Street School attained both objectives at five levels.

Central administration can use the data for making decisions about the ESEA, Title I schools. However, the staff of the 111th Street School also used the data in reporting achievement information to the parents and community. The attainment of the objectives attested to the effectiveness of IGE schooling. This is very important information for that community, regardless of the results from other ESEA, Title I schools.* It illustrates the second administrative purpose of test results identified earlier.

---

* The reader should not infer that reporting norm-referenced, group data is the major source of information for parents. It is only a part and, as we shall see in Chapter 8, the reporting to parents must to a large extent focus on the individual student.

Table 6.1 Summary results of attaining objectives by school. Taken from *Promising practices: a guide to replication; principal's directory* 1974. The Los Angeles City Unified School District, p. 21.

Schools Attaining Objective I
or Objective II at Three or More Grade Levels

Title I area	Schools attaining Objecive I (Percent below Q2)			Schools attaining Objective II (Month-for-month gains)		
	At 5 levels	At 4 levels	At 3 levels	At 5 levels	At 4 levels	At 3 levels
B	111th St.	Trinity	Compton Grape 112th St.	111th St. 112th St. Trinity	49th St. Grape	Compton Holmes
C/D	75th St.	97th St. 66th St.	109th St.		66th St.	Manchester 97th St. Parmelee 75th St.
G	Belvedere Euclid Rowan	Breed Bridge Dacotah Evergreen	Humphreys Malabar	Euclid	Belvedere Dacotah Harrison Humpheys	Bridge Brooklyn Eastman Kennedy Malabar 2nd St. Soto
N			Angeles Mesa Menlo 37th St.		36th St. Pacoima	Alta Loma Cortez Griffin
Totals	5	7	9	4	9	16

Publishers are not presently racing to flood the market with objective-based or criterion-referenced measures similar to the norm-referenced measures available. The problems of such a transition are great. Objectives would need to be satisfactory to most school districts. Criteria levels would need to be developed. Item pools for each objective would have to be generated and maintained. More expensively, flexibility would have to be offered to schools in regard to the selection of objectives to be measured and the formats for reporting results would need to be disseminated. All in all, the costs may be prohibitive.

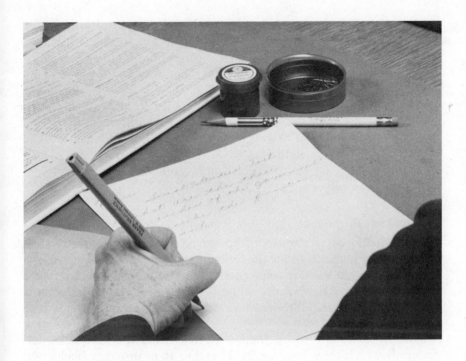

Many teachers develop tests from textbooks and other materials.

Sometimes test results are collected on a large scale for administrative purposes, and an example of that is state assessment. Not all states have state assessment programs. Some states use norm-referenced measures, and others use more objective-based instruments. In either case, these tests must be understood if they are to be useful to the school. The purpose of these tests is usually one of accountability. That is, to develop a common data base across all of the schools in the state to assist in making decisions about educational policy and resources. The content of these tests is intended to cover the basic, fundamental skills of the student. There is typically a large number of student objectives not included in such a test.

Administrators can use the results of the norm-referenced assessments to keep track of the general achievement level for schools or groups of students. This interpretation does not differ much from that done with traditional achievement tests. The major difference is that the norm group in this case includes all of the schools in the state. Perhaps this is a more meaningful norm for administrators than a national norm.

Some states have chosen objective-based assessments in an attempt to make the test results more useful to classroom teachers. Tests are then given over to at least a core of basic objectives which are common to most instructional programs. Scores are reported by objective and can then be aggregated across classrooms, schools, or districts. The greater specificity is an attempt to promote both administrative and instructional use of the test results.

The effectiveness of state assessment is still not confirmed. The extent to which these data lead to better decisions about school policy is unknown. That statewide testing is economical for instructional purposes is unlikely.

Instructional Purposes

Two instructional purposes can be served by published tests when programming instruction for the individual student. They might serve as criterion measures for some instructional objectives. They might also be used for diagnosing weaknesses or describing students as is done in Step 3 of the IPM, when specific objectives are formulated for individual students.

Many teachers develop their objectives from the textbooks and materials which they have available rather than ordering books and materials which are relevant to their objectives. Regardless of which came first, the materials or the objectives, many currently used curriculum materials contain tests or testlike exercises. Hence, these measuring instruments are widely used in practice, but rarely discussed in books about educational testing. Are these tests usually better than teacher-made tests? How reliable are these tests? What do we know about these tests? Are they appropriate for use as criterion instruments used with instructional objectives?

Not all books and materials are accompanied by tests or exercises. Of those which are, the quality of the tests is as varied as the quality of the materials themselves. A general description of their strengths and weaknesses may illustrate how they might be useful as tests in instruction.

1A The primary strength of textbook tests is that they almost always present test items which closely match the instruction. Hence, one might support these tests on the basis of their content validity.

1B A weakness with these tests is that the domain of content which the test items sample is never specified. In this case, the test user cannot really judge how well the items represent the domain of possible items.

2A Some tests published with curriculum materials assist the teachers with record keeping. For example, the Scholastic Book Series text *Phonics Two* (1973) includes a progress chart that can be filed in the record of individual student progress. The interesting feature of this chart is that the student's difficulties rather than the accomplishments are noted. By listing the problem words or letters, specific follow-up instruction may be indicated.

2B Unfortunately, some of these criterion tests tend to be item or instruction specific. That is, the test items are so like the instructional activities that teachers cannot be confident that learning is generalizable beyond those specific tasks.

3A If the teachers agree with the underlying philosophy and techniques of the authors of the curriculum materials, it is very likely that they would also agree with the testing rationale of those same materials. Hence, they would likely find the tests quite appropriate at least on logical grounds.

3B However, these tests are difficult to appraise on empirical grounds. It is rare to find documentation on reliability, validity, or even the difficulty level of items. The common philosophy was made clear in the manual for the Scott Foresman Reading Text (1971:20):

> "Since the emphasis in the Scott Foresman Reading Systems is on personalized instruction, and since teachers are encouraged to use the results as a teaching tool, the end of level tests will not be standardized. Schools can make their own local norms, and simple instructions for setting them up are included in the test manuals."

Without such empirical information it is hard to judge whether these tests are substantially better than those which the teachers themselves might construct.

4A A definite advantage of using these tests is that they are already constructed. Hence, a lot of test construction by the teachers is avoided. This is an especially powerful argument since the tests usually do not increase the cost of the materials.

4B The ease of using the available published tests may cause teachers to not create their own tests even when the teacher-made tests could clearly supplement the published tests and possibly be superior replacements. Teachers can frequently augment or embellish the published tests so that a fine test can be built without starting from zero.

5A Some textbooks are very objectives-oriented. Even higher level objectives, such as those in the analysis and synthesis levels, are covered by some of the testlike activities. For example, the text *Our Working World* (Senesh 1973) provides the teachers with the instructional objective, suggested study questions, the corresponding conclusion that should emerge, and what students should be able to write, list, or do.

5B Other series give less emphasis to comprehensive testing of student learning. For example, the *Appreciate Your Country* reading series (Stanchfield 1971) tests primarily for comprehension and vocabulary skills with exercises which follow the reading assignments. The brief exercises are a regular and integral part of instruction, but they are probably not extensive enough to serve as criterion measures. These exercises would, though, serve well as *part* of such a test.

What general conclusion can be drawn about the adequacy of tests published with curriculum materials? Since reliability and validity data are lacking, we cannot support their use on technical grounds. However, we recognize that because of their convenience and availability, their use will continue and likely increase. Thus, it seems necessary to urge teachers to systematically evaluate these tests. One way to do this is to logically analyze the content of the test to determine how well the items match the instructional objective. This will reveal whether just one or two aspects or dimensions are measured when the objective calls for more. Similarly, an empirical item analysis should be done. Often such an analysis will identify problem items that were not obvious in the logical analysis. Reliability might be assessed by administering the test again during the following week to determine the stability of the scores.

Even if such analyses indicate that the test seems satisfactory for its purpose, there is another possible problem. Many of these tests were originally designed to serve norm-referenced functions. That is, they should discriminate well among individuals. Just attaching a criterion point arbitrarily does not transform the test into a useful criterion-referenced measure. Other tests have been designed to be criterion-referenced tests, but the test authors may leave the selection of the criterion point to the user. Other authors provide a minimal criterion level, but rarely with an adequate rationale.

PUBLISHED CRITERION-REFERENCED MATERIALS

There are some objective-based, criterion-referenced tests which accompany published curriculum materials developed specifically for individualized instructional programs. Examples of these are the mathematics program of the Individually Prescribed Instruction program which was developed at the University of Pittsburgh, and the *Wisconsin Design for Reading Skill Development* developed at the University of Wisconsin. Programs such as these provide published criterion-referenced tests which have been used with students and which report empirical and logical information to support their claims. Using these tests is preferred over adapting textbook tests which have questionable empirical support.

One other useful source of criterion-referenced tests when programming instruction for the individual student is the Instructional Objectives Exchange (IOX).* This organization develops and collects tests which are linked to instructional objectives. The tests are refined, supporting data are gathered, and the results are made available to schools. It is useful for schools which are engaged in individualized, objective-based, programs to be familiar with the holdings and services of the Instructional Objectives Exchange.

Published Criterion-Referenced Tests—Examples

Consider examples of two tests selected from the IOX materials. The tests deal with language arts skills, specifically those relative to outlining. The first test (Number 6) which deals with the correct form for outlining, is as follows:

```
Test #6. Outlining: Correct form

      Objective: The student will select the correct
                 outline form from three alternatives,
                 two of which have not been indented,
                 labeled, or capitalized correctly.

      Sample item:

            Directions: In the space provided, write
                        the letter of the outline that
                        follows proper outline form.
```

---

*   The Instructional Objectives Exchange is based in Los Angeles, California. The two example tests presented here are from IOX Objectives-Based tests; Test Manual: Composition, Library and Literary Skills (Grades K-8). Los Angeles, CA., Instructional Objectives Exchange, 1973.

Example:

A	B	C

I. Fruits
  A. Apples
  B. Oranges
II. Vegetables
  A. Carrots
  B. Peas
	I. Fruits
	  1. Apples
	  2. Oranges
	II. Vegetables
	  1. Carrots
	  2. Peas
		I. fruits
		  A. apples
		  B. oranges
		II. vegetables
		  A. carrots
		  B. peas

Amplified Objective:

Testing Situation.

1. The student will be given three alternative forms of the same outline, only one of which is correct in indentation, labeling, and capitalization, and will be asked to write the letter matching the correct outline in the space provided.

2. Examples of outlining given to the student may begin at any level of specificity, i.e., need not begin with the initial Roman numeral.

3. Vocabulary will be familiar to a fourth or fifth grade pupil.

Response Alternatives.

1. Three alternatives will be given, all of which include the same information in the same order. All elements of the outline except those mentioned below in Response Alternatives #2 will be correctly given, i.e., periods after labeling letter or numeral, no single member of a hierarchy given.

2. Incorrect answers will lack all necessary capitalization at the beginning words in the outline, will lack indentation or be indented improperly, or will contain incorrect hierarchical arrangement of Roman numerals,

uppercase letters, Arabic numerals, and
lowercase letters.

<u>Criterion of Correctness.</u> The correct answer will
be the outline form which indents each group of
labels according to the following form, which
properly arranges the hierarchical labels according
to the following form, and which capitalizes the
first letter of all words in the outline.

```
 I. Xxxxxxx
    A. Xxxxxxx
       1. Xxxxxxx
       2. Xxxxxxx
    B. Xxxxxxx
II. Xxxxxxx
    A. Xxxxxxx
    B. Xxxxxxx
       1. Xxxxxxx
          a. Xxxxxxx
          b. Xxxxxxx
             i. Xxxxxxx
            ii. Xxxxxxx
       2. Xxxxxxx
```

Note that the test has an instructional objective which is, of
course, the objective covered by the test. The specific student behavior, "select," is identified in the objective. A sample item is provided.
The amplified objective heading contains under it an elaboration of
the testing situation, the response alternatives, and the criterion of
correctness.

The detail of the subheadings under amplified objective is brief
but comprehensive. The testing situation has considerable flexibility,
for example the options on the level of specificity, yet the information
is complete enough so that there is no question about the testing situation.

The response alternatives, along with the sample item, provide
for the teacher a complete model for testing. Characteristics of incorrect answers are given and the criterion of correctness is specifically
described. There should be no question about the objectivity of scoring the item.

The second test (Number 7) is concerned with categorizing and
ordering headings when outlining. It is as follows.

Test #7. Outlining: Categorizing and ordering
              headings

Objective: Given a two-paragraph selection and a
              list of headings and subheadings, some
              of which reflect the main points in
              the selection, the student will place
              appropriate headings and subheadings
              into an outline form to reflect the
              order and structure of the selection's
              content.

Sample item:

Directions: Read the selection below. Then fill in
              the skeleton outline by selecting
              headings and subheadings from the list
              provided.

Example: Stories don't happen easily. A story
              grows from an idea in a story that
              can make you smile or laugh or feel
              sad. By using certain words and
              sentences to create action and
              character, the author brings his idea
              to life. The idea is called the theme
              of the story; the kinds of words and
              sentences the author uses to express
              his idea is called his style.
                 The story is written and sent to the
              publisher, where an editor makes
              corrections. The editor sends his
              suggestions to the writer. When these
              suggestions have been considered, the
              author sends his story back to the
              publisher to be printed.

              List of topics:

              Publishing a story
              Editor's corrections
              Stories not easy to write
              Begins with an idea or theme
              Story printed
              Idea called a theme

Ideas brought to life through writer's
  style
Feeling sad or happy
Author considers editor's corrections
Words and sentences called style
The way stories grow

I. The way stories grow
   A. Begins with an idea or theme
   B. Ideas brought to life through
      writer's style
II. Publishing a story
   A. Editor's corrections
   B. Author considers editor's
      corrections
   C. Story printed

Amplified objective

Testing situation.

1. The student will be given a two-paragraph
   selection and a list of headings and subheadings,
   some of which reflect the main points in the
   selection, and will be asked to place the
   appropriate headings and subheadings into a given
   outline form to reflect the order and structure
   of the selection's content.

2. Individual paragraphs may contain no more than
   ten sentences.

3. The given skeleton outline will demand no more
   than two levels of specificity.

4. Vocabulary will be familiar to a fifth or sixth
   grade pupil.

Response alternatives.

1. Response alternatives will be phrases or clauses
   pertaining to material mentioned in the
   paragraphs. They may be taken directly from the
   text, or they may be summaries of the information
   given.

2. There will be ten or eleven headings or
   subheadings given, from which the student will
   choose the correct six or seven.

Criterion of correctness. The correct answer will be
a heading, entered beside the Roman numeral I. or
II., if the alternative paraphrases the main idea
conveyed by the topic sentence of the paragraph. The
correct answer will be a subheading, entered beside
the letters A., B., or C., if the alternative
paraphrases a secondary idea developed in the
paragraph. The order in which the headings and
subheadings are written in the outline must reflect
the order of the given selection.

The second test has the same format and level of detail as the
first test. Note that the objective is somewhat longer in wording than
the objective of the first test. The sample item is quite long, due to
the nature of the objective covered, but none of the objectivity in
scoring is lost. The two illustrative tests would most likely be appropriate for an upper primary or intermediate I & R Unit in an IGE
school.

The IOX tests illustrated are relatively short and their suggested
method of interpretation is clearly criterion-referenced. Test content
is straightforward and the arrangements and use of the tests in a
package are discussed in the test manual. How useful are such tests
to teachers programming instruction for the individual student?

The tests in themselves look highly usable, but only to the extent
that the instructional objectives coincide with those in the test. However, the objectives of the IOX are quite commonly used objectives.
Therefore, the items tend to have considerable applicability.

The tests of the IOX lend themselves well to individualized instruction. One reason for this is that they are criterion-referenced.
Another reason is that they are relatively short and can be used in
numerous combinations to reflect individual testing needs.

Supplementary and Diagnostic Information

When programming instruction for the individual student, the usefulness of tests is not limited to the actual instruction. Tests also prove
useful prior to implementing instruction, the point which corresponds
to Step 3 of the IPM of IGE. At this step the teachers use a variety

of measures to assess the student so that appropriate individual objectives might be formulated. Virtually any characteristic of the student might be measured at this step. And naturally, there are published tests available which purport to measure virtually every characteristic. The quality and usefulness of these measures have been reviewed in the *Mental Measurement Yearbooks*. Test users who are interested in using these instruments should read carefully the pertinent reviews. Those users who are interested in instruments which have not been reviewed in the *Mental Measurement Yearbook* or in reputable journals such as the *Journal of Educational Measurement, Educational and Psychological Measurement*, and the like, should proceed cautiously. The standards for reliability, validity, and usability apply in this situation as well.

It must be emphasized again that there are poor published tests and there are excellent published tests. The test selector has a great responsibility to do the job well. It is also true that the information gleaned from a published test must be better than a corresponding teacher-made test to warrant the extra cost. Some of the commonly available tests are listed in Table 6.2. The list is not exhaustive, nor is it intended to identify the best or worst of the lot; the tests are merely a representative sample.

Table 6.2 Samplings of published tests within types.

Achievement Batteries	*Intelligence*
California Achievement Tests	Stanford-Binet
Comprehensive Tests of Basic Skills	Wechsler Intelligence Scale for Children
Metropolitan Achievement Test	
Iowa Test of Basic Skills	Lorge-Thorndike Intelligence Tests
Stanford Achievement Tests	Henmon-Nelson Tests of Mental Ability
	Primary Mental Abilities Test

Reading Tests	*Special Aptitude*
Durrel Analysis of Reading Difficulty	Drake Musical Aptitude Tests
Gray Oral Reading Test	Pimsleur Language Aptitude Battery
Lee-Clark Reading Test	Differential Aptitude Tests
Nelson-Denny Reading Test	Meier Art Judgment Test
Traxler Silent Reading Test	Torrance Tests of Creative Thinking

Interest	*Personality*
Strong Vocational Interest Blank	Mooney Problems Checklist
Kuder Preference Record	Gordon Personal Profile
Ohio Vocational Interest Survey	Minnesota Multiphasic Personality
School Interest Inventory	Inventory
Minnesota Vocational Interest In-	Rorschach Ink-blot Test
ventory	Edwards Personal Preference
	Schedule

SUMMARY

The purpose of this chapter was to introduce the uses of published tests in individualizing instruction. There is a large number of published tests available which may supplement the teacher-made tests in many instructional situations. Tests can also be used for administrative purposes and these purposes were briefly discussed.

A cautious use of these instruments has been emphasized. Criteria for selecting published tests have been listed, and strengths and weaknesses of published tests in general have been stated. A careful consideration of the content of this chapter should cause teachers to want both an empirical and logical rationale for the published tests that they use. It is also hoped that teachers themselves will statistically analyze results from published tests so that those tests which lack empirical credentials will be properly evaluated.

DISCUSSION TOPICS

1. Which of the textbooks that you presently use provide chapter or unit tests? How adequate are the supporting data for these tests?

2. What should be the primary technical considerations for selecting a published test on arithmetic achievement? on perceptual difficulties?

3. What are some of the nontechnical considerations of published tests that teachers feel strongly about?

4. What are the advantages and disadvantages of using performance on a published test as the criterion task in an instructional objective?

REFERENCES

American Psychological Association 1974. *Standards for Educational and Psychological Tests*, Washington, D.C.

Buros, O. K. 1975. The eighth *mental measurements yearbook*, Highland Park, N.J.: Gryphon.

———— 1961. *Tests in print,* Highland Park, N.J.: Gryphon.

Flournoy, L. P. 1974. *Promising practices: a guide to replication; principal's directory.* Report prepared by the Los Angeles City Unified School District, 1974.

Manual Level 2 1971. "Scott Foresman reading text," Glenview, Ill.: Scott Foresman.

Phonics Two 1973. New York: Scholastic Book Service.

Senesh, L. 1973. *Teachers resource guide for our working world.* Chicago: Science Research Associates.

Stanchfield, J. 1971. *Appreciate your country; reading series.* San Francisco: Learning Communications.

7
Evaluating Instructional Programs

Objectives

After reading this chapter, the reader will be able:

- To identify differences between evaluating student progress and evaluating the effects of instructional programs.

- To identify data from students and other sources that can be used to evaluate instructional programs.

- To explain the need for evaluating the program requirements, implementation, and results.

- To understand how evaluating the instructional program can be coordinated across all units.

Most traditional textbooks in measurement and evaluation concentrate on either evaluating student learning or on evaluating the effect of a program or curriculum. In the context of instructional programming for the individual student, we use "programs" in the plural since several instructional programs are developed for one student. Therefore, the instruction that takes place is not viewed as a single program applicable to all students. A published curriculum program, for example, is not considered a single program, but if content from such a program is used, it is applied appropriately for the instructional programs of the individual students.

We have chosen to include evaluation of instructional programs in this book for two reasons. First, formative evaluation is stressed here. The purpose of formative evaluation is to identify strengths and weaknesses in developing instructional programs so that improvement can be continuous. The people who are closest to instructional programs, the teachers, are in the best position to provide an accurate description of the students and the instruction. The second reason for including this chapter is that the persons who are responsible for improving instructional programs are the teachers. Hence, it is important that teachers understand the purpose and procedures of evaluation so that they will participate in it and make it work as effectively as possible.

PURPOSE OF PROGRAM EVALUATION

The purpose of evaluating instructional programs, as discussed in this chapter, is for improving the instruction of the students. It is not an attempt to evaluate teachers for administrative reasons. Decisions about salaries, tenure, and other similar matters should not be seen as a focus of this chapter. It is essential to separate those administrative concerns from instructional concerns. If such a separation is not made, the teachers involved may naturally tend to avoid quantification and discussion of some important variables.

This distinction is important enough to warrant the determination of policies and procedures in each I & R Unit. The teachers should establish at the outset who will have access to which data. They should also consider the discussions and decisions that will be based on their evaluation. For example, if the evaluation revealed that a small set of objectives was taking up an inordinate amount of instructional time, the teachers should consider changing either the objectives or the instructional strategies. These data need not be shared with administrators. Instead, the teachers can discuss the situation and propose changes which might improve the instructional programs within the I & R Unit.

Program evaluation actually proceeds in much the same way that decisions about students are made. Data are gathered to see whether the instruction and its resultant student outcomes meet the teachers' expectations. Supporting data are gathered so that when deficiencies are found, corrective action can be based on diagnosed weaknesses rather than on hunches or whims.

The domains of objectives for student learning have been described as the cognitive, affective, and psychomotor domains. Similarly, there are three major aspects which should be included in the evaluation of instructional programs. These are the *program requirements*, the *program implementation*, and the *program results*. A description of the purposes and techinques of these three components will clarify the kinds of decisions that are facilitated by the evaluation of the instructional program.

EVALUATION OF THE PROGRAM REQUIREMENTS

The evaluation of the program requirements includes a variety of elements. Readers who are familiar with the literature of educational evaluation will find the term similar to "Antecedents" in Stake's model (Stake 1967) or "Input" in Stufflebeam's Context-Input-Process-Product (Stufflebeam 1971). In essence, this part of the total evaluation explores the rationale for the instructional programs and the level of resources which the programs require.

The specificity and level of detail in this part of the evaluation is often a judgment which the instructional staff can make according to the nature of their own programs. More detail is needed for emergent programs while established programs would more likely concentrate on the implementation and results parts of the evaluation.

THE PURPOSE OF EVALUATING PROGRAM REQUIREMENTS

There are two major reasons for evaluating program requirements. The first is to determine whether the description and rationale of the intended programs are supported by the instructional staff and by the community. Once the intended programs are understood and conceptually accepted, the second purpose is to determine whether or not the instructional staff can implement the programs and, if not, how close the staff is to implementation.

The first part of the evaluation of program requirements occurs when the instructional staff compares alternative models for conducting instruction. Such a comparison would include classroom management, grouping patterns, making decisions about individual students, instructional materials and a variety of other concerns. A logical rationale for programs, which is consistent with the philosophy for that particular school, would certainly be essential.

Once the rationale and designs for instructional programs are selected or tailored to the specific needs of the school, then the required resources can be identified. The number and kinds of teachers, aides, and other supportive personnel that are necessary for optional programs can be compared to the present staff so that any needs are identified. Similarly, any inservice needs should be recognized so that the existing staff can be trained to the level which is required for implementing the instructional programs. The instructional materials and other program needs would also be noted.

The result of evaluating program requirements is a decision about how capable the instructional staff is to implement the programs in the manner intended. This decision will be based on a comparison on the program's needs and the levels of support and expertise of the staff.

Example of Evaluation of Program Requirements

An example of a program requirements evaluation is seen in the efforts of Elementary School District 96 in Long Grove, Illinois (Jurs 1973). Once it was decided that the district would adapt the programs so that instruction would be programmed for the individual student, that is, once IGE began to be implemented, an assessment was made about the discrepancy between the present level at which the staff was functioning and the level necessary for full implementation of the desired instructional programs. Objectives were set which were designed to overcome these discrepancies. An inservice program for developing the staff and orientation meetings were held so that the instructional staff would understand and contribute to the transition necessary for implementing IGE.

As inservice was being conducted and initial implementation activities were taking place, evaluation data were collected periodically to monitor progress toward attaining objectives. Data in this case were collected by an outside consultant but they could also be collected by a committee of building staff, or by the IIC if it were already functional. What follows is a listing of data on selected objectives four months after inservice began. The "other" category refers to written comments describing a position somewhere between yes and no.

Teachers need to evaluate instructional objectives for individual students.

The objectives for the school in preparing for implementation, and the progress made toward those objectives are as follows (objectives are numbered):

1. The administrative staff organized units composed of Unit Leader, Unit Teachers, Aides, and Students.

	Yes	No	Other
Willow Grove	28	3	0
Kildeer	23	0	0
Total	51	3	0

2. Units consist of students of at least two age levels with approximately equal numbers at each age level.

	Yes	No	Other
Willow Grove	8	22	1
Kildeer	1	20	2
Total	9	42	3

3. Administrators assess the performance of units in terms of unit objectives and provide appropriate feedback.

	Yes	No	Other
Willow Grove	10	16	5
Kildeer	10	7	6
Total	20	23	11

4. Administrators have specified the inservice needs of the staff.

	Yes	No	Other
Willow Grove	30	0	1
Kildeer	20	1	2
Total	50	1	3

5. Unit teachers make the decisions about time, space, materials, staff, and students.

	Yes	No	Other
Willow Grove	26	5	0
Kildeer	20	0	3
Total	46	5	3

6. Continuous progress charts monitor the student progress through the instructional objectives.

	Yes	No	Other
Willow Grove	11	14	6
Kildeer	6	9	8
Total	17	23	14

7. Students often select their own learning objectives.

	Yes	No	Other
Willow Grove	5	23	3
Kildeer	2	17	4
Total	7	40	7

8. Students often select their own learning activities.

	Yes	No	Other
Willow Grove	17	9	5
Kildeer	14	6	3
Total	31	15	8

9. Materials have been developed which include: (a) broad goals, (b) preassessment, (c) performance objectives, (d) learning activities, (e) postassessment, (f) recycle options.

	Yes	No	Other
Kildeer	12	4	7
Total	28	17	9
Willow Grove	16	13	2

10. Teachers have written performance objectives for all broad educational goals.

	Yes	No	Other
Willow Grove	12	16	3
Kildeer	13	5	5
Total	25	21	8

11. Teachers have developed a selection of learning activities for each of the performance objectives.

	Yes	No	Other
Willow Grove	14	13	4
Kildeer	14	5	4
Total	28	18	8

While the performance data above were being collected, the attitudes of the staff toward the transition to IGE were also being assessed. The strengths and weaknesses of the emergent program were noted. This allowed the administrators to sense the "pulse" of the staff during the program development. Examples of the teachers' comments relative to strengths and weaknesses appear. It can be seen that the transition was professionally demanding, but the teachers generally supported the change.

Strengths

I feel that the strength of the curriculum lies in the spirit of working with people who understand it, enjoy the flexibility of working with it, and who share a common philosophy of its implementation.

I feel that the team has really banded together to work with the children in the most beneficial and individualized approach to learning. My team's efforts have been proved to be most satisfying to the teachers and the children involved.

As the year has progressed our team cooperation has gotten better and better. The whole staff seems to be working together much better. For myself, I am very excited and eager about next year.

I see greater communication within a team. We are on the road to individualizing but we have a way to go. We do not feel free enough as yet. Communication with my administrators is good.

Teachers are presently working on objectives for next year. I feel there is much more cooperation among teachers not only within units but among units. I think teachers are excited about working in the IGE system.

Weaknesses

I never have enough time, even yet, to do all I would like to do. I still get anxious about the program because I have never done it before and there is so much I need to know.

Many "bugs" to be worked out—revisions will be forthcoming—some trial and error will be going on, but is this necessarily a weakness?

Total communication, up and down, is a constant problem, as much as we try to improve it. I don't know for sure if everyone on the staff understands the total *concept* of an IGE planning system.

A great deal to do and not enough time in which to get it all done.

We are still experimenting and make a lot of mistakes. Confusion often reigns.

AN EVALUATION OF PROGRAM IMPLEMENTATION

Once the instructional program is in operation, it is necessary for the instructional staff to monitor instruction to determine whether it is consistent with intended IGE implementation. Other authors have called this a "process evaluation" or the evaluation of the classroom "transactions."

It is often useful to list a set of process objectives for this evaluation similar to the program objectives that were discussed in the preceding section. For example, the following list contains some of the general process objectives that were developed for the evaluation of the IGE implementation project at Martin Luther King, Jr., School in Toledo, Ohio (Jurs and Wysong 1973, p. 235).

1. Students spend more time in instructional activities, receive more individualized instruction time, receive more variety in educational experiences, receive more individual attention.
2. All staff members of the unit carry out their responsibilities in the unit.
3. The IIC makes decisions that support the units.
4. Principal, counselor, resource staff, and the IIC serve one another.
5. Units assist parents and community to understand growth of children in IGE.

Other general process objectives could easily be written. Of course, each of these must be expanded and defined more specifically to fit the needs of each particular school.

Purpose of Evaluating the Implementation

The purpose of evaluating the implementation of the designed programs is to determine whether they are, in fact, implemented in a manner consistent with their design. For example, are the communication patterns, student involvement, and materials utilization which were important parts of the intended programs actually being applied in the classroom?

Results of such an evaluation should identify deficiencies which the instructional staff might be able to correct. This evaluation also serves to remind the instructional staff of its responsibility to the total instruction of the school and the interdependence of all those involved.

An Example of Evaluating IGE Implementation

Ironside (1973) has provided a process evaluation of nationwide installation of IGE schools. This was a comprehensive study involving a sampling of close to 100 schools. The detailed results of the study can be found in the report referenced at the end of the chapter.

The focus of this discussion is not on the results of the study but on part of an instrument used in evaluating the implementation process. A questionnaire was developed for use by the IIC and an extensive item from that questionnaire appears in Figure 7.1.

The 12 points, all of which include subpoints, provide a relatively comprehensive coverage of the implementation process. The kinds of questions are well suited for IIC member response. However, any unit leader on the IIC would base the input on what is happening in the I & R Units. Although the questions deal with process, they clearly relate to the quality of instruction within the units.

It might be commented, "obviously the kinds of things listed in

Figure 7.1 need to be done in implementing IGE." That may or may not be obvious to IIC members and the teachers in the I & R Units. It is important to identify the practices and to collect data on the extent to which they are being carried out. In this way deficiencies can be identified and corrected. Although, the item of Figure 7.1 was

> Schools are implementing MUS-E and IGE in
> different ways and on different sched-
> ules. As an aid in summarizing certain over-
> all practices across schools this year, please
> answer each item below with a Yes or No, indicat-
> ing present operations and features of your
> school's MUS-E/IGE implementation. Please answer
> in terms of the 1972–73 school year.

	Yes	No
1. (a) Do you hold regular IIC meetings on a scheduled basis?		
(b) Does the IIC make decisions concerning the instructional program?...........		
2. (a) Is the IMC/library adequately stocked with instructional material?		
(b) Is the IMC/library being "used to capacity" by students and teachers?....		
3. (a) In general, do teachers in the units take on different roles within the units (differentiated staffing)?		
(b) Are paraprofessionals contributing to the instructional program?...........		
4. (a) Are lines of communication in the school "open"?		
(b) Are teachers' concerns and needs considered by the IIC and principal? ...		
5. (a) Are your units multiaged (with a 2 to 4 year spread)?		
(b) Within the units, is instruction itself typically directed to multiaged groups of children?		
6. (a) Has MUS-E/IGE changed the principal's role to one of increased participation in the instructional program? ..		
(b) Has the principal been able to encourage teachers to experiment with different instructional approaches?		

	Yes	No

7. (a) Do you have at least one IGE subject at this time? ....

   (b) Is it being implemented in <u>all</u> the units? ....

   (c) Is the "instructional programming model" being followed in all the units with respect to the IGE subject? ....

8. (a) In general, are the units functioning as "working groups"? That is, are the unit staffs doing cooperative planning and teaching?...................

   (b) Do most teachers appear content with their "teammates"?...................

9. (a) Is your school fully unitized at this time? That is, are all students and regular classroom teachers in units? ....

   (b) Is the kindergarten instructionally integrated with a primary unit? ....

10. (a) Are unit leaders focusing unit attention on the IGE subject and the instructional programming model? ......

    (b) In general, are unit leaders finding it easy to encourage or assign a variety of teaching responsibilities in the units? ....

11. (a) On the whole, does the school staff appear to be "sold" on the idea of the multiunit school structure? .....

    (b) Is there a general atmosphere of commitment to individualized education among teachers at this time? ....

12. (a) Do you have periodic or regularly scheduled inservice training for the whole school staff? ....

    (b) Have school representatives attended various sorts of training and conferences sponsored by agencies outside the school since 6/72? ......

    (c) Have you called on other resources or consultants for assistance? ....

Fig 7.1 An item for the IIC dealing with the process of implementation.

The IIC provides a forum for coordinating evaluation across units.

developed in connection with a national project, the content applies to individual schools and their operation. The IIC of a school might use these kinds of items intact, or use them as a base for developing their own instruments. The process of implementation is too important to be evaluated through simple, ad hoc, oral statements.

An Example of Evaluating Implementation

An example of some of the sorts of the implementation evaluation can be seen in the description of the 111th Street School Project in Los Angeles (Flournoy 1974).

Figure 7.2 indicates one page from the school calendar. A variety of activities are listed, which are consistent with the optimally de-

week	**m**	**t**	**w**	**th**	**f**
3	CTBS Testing, Upper Age Group, and First Grade Placement Testing (State Mandated)				
	Orientation Workshop—Education Aides. Subjects include: • Objectives of 111th Street School • Proper use of equipment • Records maintenance • Student control and relationships Parents also attend training sessions to qualify as classroom volunteers.		It is the teacher's responsibility to ensure that the test environment gives every student an opportunity to do his best on this important test.	Send letters to parents re: Jr. High Articulation Program. Start Parent In-Service Training. Parents receive much the same training as paid aides. Many parents who desire to do so, go on to become paid educational aides at 111th Street School.	Instructional Improvement Committee meeting.

week	**m** VETERANS DAY	**t**	**w**	**th**	**f**
4		Post Assessment of Objectives, Team A (Early Childhood). See page 51 for procedures. Meeting of Parents Advisory Council. Start IGE Cycle One, 3-week Cycle for Upper Age Group (Ages 10, 11, 12) IGE. Learning Center Schedule Sample Set 7 to Center 1 Empty Center 2 Set 2 to Center 3 Set 3 to Center 4 Set 4 to Center 5 Set 5 to Center 6 Set 6 to Center 7 (see page 58)	Post Assessment of Objectives, Team B (Early Childhood). Parent In-Service. Teachers meet with parents at joint in-service. Rotate Sets in Home Room Learning Centers. Sets are rotated in home room centers; sets in reading and math may or may not rotate, depending on the needs of the students.	Post Assessment of Objectives, Teams A' & B' (Early Childhood). Rotate Sets in Home Room Learning Centers. 1973 Racial and Ethnic Survey Due. Parents Meeting for Jr. High Articulation Program. Parent In-Service.	End of 3-week Cycle (Early Childhood). Re-cycle Early Childhood Instruction on the Basis of Objectives Obtained. Successful students move ahead. Unsuccessful students start remedial instruction. Affective Domain Activities. See page 138 for sample objectives and staff development activities in this experimental program. Instructional Improvement Committee meeting.

week	**m** Start 3-week Cycle Upper Age Group	**t** Start second IGE cycle (Early Childhood).	**w**	**th**	**f**
5		Rotate Sets in Learning Centers			
	One teacher at 111th Street has all of her students put their heads on the table and "get themselves together" when they return from noon recess. After 5 minutes they are settled down, refreshed, and ready to go to work at their Learning Centers.	Kick-off Meeting of Student Council (Conducted by V.P.). PTA Meeting. The PTA provides an opportunity for direct involvement by parents who cannot otherwise participate in the school program. Teachers should encourage all parents to join.	Parent In-Service. Typical Home Room Learning Centers for one class: 1. Study Skills follow-up 2. Handwriting 3. Language (verb usage) 4. Spelling 5. Language (capitalization) 6. Writing (sentence structure) 7. Poetry (writing limericks)		
october					

Fig. 7.2 Facsimile page from the Calendar of the 111th Street School Project. Adapted from Flournoy 1974, p. 16.

INSTRUCTIONAL SCHEDULE

Upper Age Group

Instructional Cycle #3

(Dec. 3, 1975 to Jan. 10, 1976)

TEAMS [C-C'-D]	9:00-9:40 9:40-10:30	10:50-12:10	1:10-2:30	2:30-3:00
D 107	IGE Reading—Small group W.A. Pupils Comp. *C-16-18 15 Main Idea C-13-15 15 Conclusions D-1,2,3 15 Seg. Order	Class-size group 3 days Language / Spelling / Handwriting 2 days Study skills / Social studies / Science—health	IGE Math—Small group Pupils	Psychomotor—Large group One-to-one Small group Skills
Bates Biddle Eatis Labs. - Joseph 29 Thomas 28				
C 104	IGE Math—Small group Pupils	IGE Reading—Small group W.A. Pupils Comp. *C-4,5 12 Foll. Dir., Seq. Ord. C-6,7 12 Foll. Dir. C-8,9 12 Main Idea	Class-size group 3 days Language / Spelling / Handwriting 2 days Study Skills / Social studies / Science—health	Psychomotor—Large group One-to-one Small group Skills
Davis Chatman Jenkins Labs.- Joseph 34 Thomas 34				

C'	136	Class-size group	IGE Math—Small group	IGE Reading—Small group			Psychomotor—Large group
			Pupils	W.A.	Pupils	Comp.	One-to-one Small group
		3 days		D-1,2,3	14	Seg. Order	Skills
McNeal		Language		C'-8	16	Seg. Order	
Lee		Spelling		D-1,2,3	14	Seg. Order	
Williams, G.		Handwriting		C'-10	.16	Main Idea	
Marshall							
		2 days					
Labs. - Joseph 38		Study skills					
Thomas 38		Social studies					
		Science—health					

RESOURCES

Music: Fitzgerald
Horizontal Organization of
Reading Skills:
—Dance
—Orchestra
—Chorus
—Drama

Large Groups
Small Groups
Class-size Groups
One-to-one

Reading Skill Development
   Thomas
   Joseph
Education Aides
  Stickney Matthews
  Hill   Donahue
  Moland Johnson

Developmental Math Process Educational Resource Center
  E. Erwin   J. Cohn
Psychomotor
  W. Kimball

Total enrollment 347

* Refers to IGE Skill Card on Word Attack

Fig. 7.3 Facsimile lesson plan which allows for evaluation of curriculum implementation. Adapted from Flournoy 1974, p. 59.

signed instructional programs. It is easy for the evaluators, in this case the instructional staff, to note whether the calendar was adhered to; that is, whether the planned activities actually took place.

Similarly, lesson plans can be collected to determined whether they are consistent with the designed programs. Observers can be used to note whether the written lesson plans are really followed. An example of such a lesson plan appears in Figure 7.3.

Minutes of IIC meetings would also provide a useful record for evaluators. The frequency of meetings and the nature of the topics covered would indicate how effective these meetings were for facilitating communication across the units.

The results of the evaluation of the implementation should show whether the program is operating as it was intended. If deficiencies are determined, it is the responsibility of the instructional staff to take the appropriate action to correct the situation.

EVALUATING THE RESULTS OF THE PROGRAMS

This part of the evaluation of instructional programs is perhaps the most important part of all. Certainly, it is the part that receives the most publicity. Most of the data on which this evaluation is based are contained in the record of student progress across the instructional objectives. The primary concern of this evaluation is how well the students learned in all areas, cognitive, affective, and psychomotor. Other outcomes such as cost, teacher attitudes, and unintended side effects should be monitored too, but they do not have the salience of the objectives-based student growth.

There are several ways to interpret student growth. Growth rates might be compared to some present criterion, or to that of a control group, or even to their own predicted growth.

In terms of comparison to a preset criterion, the evaluator might merely aggregate the performances of groups of students across sets of objectives to determine how students did relative to teacher expectations. An example of how such aggregating of data might be done appears in Figure 7.4.

Note that in the form of Figure 7.4, student performance is tied to the attainment of objectives. Attainment may mean mastery of the objective, but this is not necessarily required of all objectives. In some cases attainment may mean making progress toward reaching the criterion of the objective. Also, with certain objectives such as some expressive objectives, participation in a given activity may constitute attainment of the objective.

The most recent score might represent performance on a test or

Individual Performance Records

Objective	Student	Most recent score	Number attempts	Objective attained
0–16	A. Bartlett	36	2	√
0–16	J. Clemenson	38	1	√
0–16	P. Rieger	38	1	√
0–17	W. Oldefendt	27	2	
0–18	D. Walker	45	3	
0–19	M. Roths	16	1	
.	.	.	.	.
.	.	.	.	.
.	.	.	.	.

Aggregated Performance Records

Objective	Number of students attaining objective on 1st attempt	Number of students attaining objective on 2nd attempt	Number of students who have yet to attain this objective
0–16	27	3	0
0–17	20	10	0
0–18	21	2	0
0–19	17	8	5
0–20	15	5	5
.	.	.	.
.	.	.	.
.	.	.	.

Fig. 7.4 Aggregating student performance scores from individual scores.

work sample, for example. In some instances there may not be a score, simply an indicator of progress or participation. Then that column could simply be checked. So, there is considerable flexibility in recording data in the form.

An Example of Evaluating Program Results

A study illustrating how actual achievement scores might be compared to predicted scores was done by Gervose and Lindia (1974). They predicted reading performance for the students in IGE of the Windsor Public Schools, Windsor, Connecticut, using the Bond and Tinker formula. Statistics were then calculated to determine whether the actual average reading scores of the students were significantly better than the predicted average. In each comparison in this study the reading performance of the students in IGE averaged significantly better than their expected scores.

The results of such an evaluation would clearly lead to a decision to continue and expand the implementation of IGE because of the evidence for its success.

Other Important Results

Although the scores from performances related to the instructional objectives provide the most important student data in the evaluation of instructional programs, other kinds of student data are also useful. Often, there will be a need for affective data even though there may be no specific affective objectives. For example, it may be useful to determine how students perceived particular materials or teaching strategies. Teachers can also gain insight by assessing the motivation or anxiety level of the students when a new approach is used. These data can be gathered through the use of checklists or rating scales as discussed in Chapter 4.

Other data from students include unobtrusive measures of the side effects of instruction. For example, instruction on dinosaurs may kindle interests to a point where some students read about dinosaurs during free time periods. Other students might bring models of diplodoci or protoceratopses to school. Such behavior illustrates the success of the instruction. But if these outcomes are not stated in the instructional objectives, it is quite likely that this evidence will be lost. Keeping track of such unintended side effects allows teachers to document the effectiveness of their instruction.

The side effects of instruction can sometimes be more potent than the instruction. A demanding mathematics lesson might be taught in such an intimidating manner as to "turn off" students even though the cognitive achievement on the related objective was judged to be satisfactory.

Other kinds of information should also be considered even though they are not student outcomes. Surely the effects of instruction on the teachers, administrators, and parents should be considered in any evaluation of the instructional program. When students achieve equally well in two different instructional situations, the choice might best be based on the preferences of the teachers. Administrators, counselors, and parents can also give useful insights into the effects of the instructional programs when it is impossible for teachers to observe. For example, the dinner conversations, the kinds of play activities, and comments made to counselors may all offer clues about the effects of instruction. For some of these effects, the parents are in the best position to bring information to the teachers' attention.

Another kind of data that might be considered is cost. "You get what you pay for" is not a phrase that makes sense in education. Time and again it has been shown that there is no direct link between the amount of money that is spent and the level of student learning. Hence, it is the responsibility of the teachers and administrators to use their fiscal resources wisely. Curricula materials can be evaluated in terms of dollars when alternative choices do not result in different levels of student learning.

COORDINATING EVALUATION ACROSS I & R UNITS

The evaluation procedures presented here are concerned with three parts of a total evaluation program; that is, the kind of formative evaluation that might be done by the principal and teachers of an IGE school. The purpose is not to label the instructional programs good or bad, better or worse than other programs, or cost-effective. The purpose has been to systematically gather data in such a way that the strong and weak points of the programs can be identified. Hopefully, this kind of evaluation will produce orderly improvement. The teachers themselves are charged with the evaluation responsibilities because their involvement is more likely to lead to actually making improvements based on the evaluation results. This would not be so if evaluation came from some external source, although in some cases consultants may assist in preparing measuring instruments and collecting data.

One way to build the evaluation component into the school program is to delegate responsibility for the different activities across the several units in the school. The IIC of a school is responsible for dealing with evaluation concerns at the school level and for any coordination of evaluation activities across units.

Although the unit staffs will probably have few specific objectives in common, they have similar data needs such as student attitudes, parents' perceptions, and cost considerations. It may be more efficient to be consistent in measuring these variables so that meaningful comparisons can be made across units. This also eliminates some duplication of effort if these measures are developed cooperatively.

Another important result of coordinating the evaluation across the several units is that it is helpful in planning future instruction if similar results occur in several units. For example, if all units report that they are unsatisfied with their tests of student "independence," then a cooperative effort might be launched to improve those measures. Similarly, by sharing evaluation results, the mistakes of some units might be avoided by other units. This kind of sharing can be very productive, but it can also be very threatening. It is a threat if the evaluation results are used for administrative functioning, for example, for granting tenure. It is productive sharing if the evaluation results are used to attain a common goal—the improvement of instructional programs.

SUMMARY

There is a definite need for integrating evaluation responsibilities with the instructional efforts. A close and continuous link should result in improvement of both the instruction and the evaluation. The evaluation can be focused narrowly or broadly, but the data gathered must be adequate for diagnosing weaknesses in the instructional programs as they are being implemented.

The various procedures discussed in this chapter should assist teachers to evaluate both the objectives of instructional programs and the instruction in the programs. School-level evaluation activities should provide some coordination of evaluation efforts, and these activities should be directed toward improving instruction.

DISCUSSION TOPICS

1. Should different people conduct the evaluations of program requirements, program implementation, and program results?
2. How should the instrument construction, data gathering, data analysis, and data interpretation responsibilities be shared within a unit?
3. What policies need to be developed about what data should be collected, what data should be saved, who should be allowed to see the data, etc.?
4. What problems are there when one compares achievement to: (1) a criterion, (2) a control group, and (3) a predicted score?

REFERENCES

Flournoy, L. P. 1974. *Promising practices: a guide to replication, classroom directory, One Hundred Eleventh Street School.* Los Angeles: Los Angeles Unified School District.

Gervase, C. J. and A. Lindia 1974. *Final report—the evaluation of the IGE program in the Windsor Public Schools (Reading).* (Unpublished report.) Windsor, Conn.: Board of Education.

Ironside, R. A. 1973. *A supplement to the 1971–1972 nationwide installation of the multiunit/IGE model for elementary schools,* Princeton: Educational Testing Service.

Jurs, S. G. 1973. *Evaluation of implementation of IGE in elementary district 96.* (Unpublished report.)

————, and H. E. Wysong 1973. Evaluation and feedback for CBTE and IGE/MUS. In G. E. Dickson, R. W. Saxe, *et al. Partners for educational reform and renewal.* Berkeley: McCutchan.

Stake, R. E. 1967. The countenance of educational evaluation. *Teachers College Record* **68**:523–540.

Stufflebeam, D., *et al.* 1971. *Educational evaluation and decision making.* Itasca, Ill.: Peacock.

8
Recording and Reporting Pupil Progress

Objectives

After reading this chapter, the reader will be able:

- To understand the functions of keeping records for individual and group performance.
- To know various formats for systematic record keeping.
- To understand procedures for reporting to parents, both written and verbal.

Systematic record keeping is essential. Any instructional system lacking sound record-keeping procedures tends to become fragmented, repetitious, and noncommunicative. Record keeping requires certain resources, especially time, but it is well worth the effort with the payoff in sound, instructional management.

FUNCTIONS OF SYSTEMATIC RECORD KEEPING

In a general sense, record keeping provides a base for reporting pupil learning and progress. But pupil progress is reported and used in several different contexts. Within the I & R Unit in IGE, progress is reported to the student. Reporting progress also takes place within the school, between teachers and parents, and within the school system. Therefore, it is useful to divide record keeping into specific functions depending upon the uses of pupil progress information.

Primary Function

The primary function of record keeping, when using objective-based instruction for the individual student, is to provide a continuous record of the instructional objectives which have and have not been met by each student. In IGE this function is conducted within the unit itself. Assessment is based directly on the instructional objectives. Therefore, the record of pupil progress should clearly indicate where the pupil is in attaining the learning outcomes (skills, knowledge, etc.) in a sequence of instructional objectives.

When using criterion-referenced assessment, the major emphasis is on the student's having met the criteria of the instructional objectives in an absolute sense. That is, has the student attained the criteria of the instructional objectives regardless of the performance of others? However, it is usually the case that information is also provided relative to the performance of students in the group and in some cases information on the grade level performance of the student if traditional curriculum materials are being used.*

Records on the attainment of instructional objectives should also contain information about other instructional factors. Information about the motivational level of the student may be available. There may be suggestions about learning style or techniques most appropriate for instruction. Suppose a student does not meet one or more of the instructional objectives. Information should be available that will lead to instruction that enables the student to meet the objectives.

---

* See, for example, the *Wisconsin Design for Reading Skill Development,* 1972, Madison, Wisc.: The University of Wisconsin—Madison.

Students who require instruction related to one or more objectives can be appropriately grouped with relevant instructional methods and materials. Thus, the information in the records should be useful for continuing instruction, and not be limited to simply deciding whether or not instructional objectives have been met.

Other Functions

Record keeping serves as a valuable means of communication between the various individuals or groups concerned with pupil progress. The record keeping in itself does not provide the communication but it does provide the basis for intelligent and useful communication.

Communication between teacher and student. This communication is closely related to the primary function of record keeping—to provide a visible means of informing students of their individual progress. Used properly, records can serve effectively as a motivating device for the student. In any event, when implemented properly, instructional programming for the individual student includes having the students know what is expected of them and how they are doing.

Communication between teacher and teacher. Since the student in IGE has interchange with the several teachers in the unit, it is important to have an efficient means of keeping teachers informed about the student's progress. It is hardly adequate to rely on informal or ad hoc conversation between teachers. The records provide an efficient and objective means of informing all teachers of the unit about student progress. Other school personnel such as the principal or aide can also refer to the records.

Communication between teacher and parent. The communication between teacher and parent may be somewhat different in level of professional sophistication than that between teachers, but it should still be based on an objective record of student progress. It would be difficult for a teacher to defend claims not supported by information. Also, parents usually want to know specifics about their child's progress, not some vague generalizations. More comments will be provided later in the chapter when communication with parents and the forms such communication can take are discussed.

PROCEDURES OF SYSTEMATIC RECORD KEEPING

There are any number of specific procedures, forms, etc., that can be used for recording student data, especially performance data. Some curriculum materials have record-keeping devices that accompany the materials. These can be supplemented by teacher-constructed devices or systems.

In this section, examples will be presented illustrating systematic record keeping. These examples will include devices used with specific curriculum materials as well as those having more general application. Not all information in the records consists of student test data. Information can come from work samples, rating scales, anecdotal records and the like.

Relating Performance to Objectives—Self-constructed Forms

Student performance data generally consist of scores on test items, work samples, etc. One way of recording information is simply to indicate whether or not the objective has been attained. But usually the test results can be more specifically tied to the objectives. Figure 8.1 presents a report form for relating the results of one or more tests to the attainment of the objectives covered by the test.

Instead of listing the objectives, the form simply lists the learning outcomes required by the objectives. The number in parentheses following the learning outcome gives the number of test items related to the learning outcome. Usually, there are several items related to a learning outcome or objective.

With criterion-referenced testing there must be an identifiable criterion that indicates that the objective has been attained. The criterion would not necessarily indicate mastery, it might indicate a desired change in direction or a level of achievement that represents progress toward mastery. Suppose that for the objectives in the figure, attainment of the objective is indicated by having at least 85 percent of the relevant test items correct.

Including the percent of items correct not only indicates directly whether or not the objective has been attained, but also aids in interpreting the performance. For example, lack of attaining the objective is interpreted differently if 70 percent correct rather than 10 percent correct had been the result.

The kind of form presented in Figure 8.1 can be used conveniently for a single test or possibly a small number of tests. When all the objectives for several content areas for a period of time are to be considered, a summary form such as that shown in Figure 8.2 can be used. In this form the objectives are listed by number in order to condense the listing.

The information in the form of Figure 8.2 is somewhat different from that of Figure 8.1. The extent of progress toward attaining the objective is shown and, if mastery is the criterion, this can also be in-

| Test *Science* | Student | *John Doe* | |
Objective or Learning Outcome	Number correct	Percent correct	Objective attained
1. Knows basic scientific terms (10)	7	70	No
2. Knows scientific symbols (15)	14	93	Yes
3. Applies scientific principles (9)	8	89	Yes
.	.	.	.
.	.	.	.
.	.	.	.
.	.	.	.

Fig. 8.1 Report form for relating test performance to the mastery of objectives. Adapted from Gronlund 1973.

dicated. However, for some objectives complete mastery may not be required for attaining the objective. The value of the form in Figure 8.2 is in providing a summary across content areas. It does not provide diagnostic information from test items.

One disadvantage of the form in Figure 8.2 is that if large numbers of instructional objectives are used and if the period covered is quite long, the form will become long and cumbersome. It may be possible to group objectives rather than consider each singly and in this way shorten the form. Self-constructed forms can be manipulated and revised in any way that enhances their usefulness.

Additional forms for recording student performance information are provided in following sections. In the reading example recording performance related to interpretive reading skills is illustrated.

Relating Performance to Objectives—Mathematics Example

In this section we will consider forms that can be used with the objectives of *Developing Mathematical Processes* (1970). The DMP content is divided into topics and Topic 2.9, dealing with order sentences, has been selected as an example. This topic is intended for use with students six to eight years of age.

The objectives for Topic 2.9 are as follows:

1. Given an order sentence, reads it. (reads order sentence)

2. Given two objects or sets, chooses an appropriate order sentence. (chooses order sentence)

Summary of Student Performance

Name _____   Unit _____

Area	Obj. (by No.)	Pre-test	Posttest Inadequate progress	Progress	Mastery	Obj. met
Reading	1	NP	X			
.	2	NP			X	X
.	3	NP		X		X
.	.	.				
.						
.						
.						
Mathematics	1					
.	2					
.	3					
.	.					
.	.					
.	.					
.	.					
.	.					
Science	1					
.	2					
.	3					
.	.					
.	.					
.	.					

Fig. 8.2 Example form for summarizing student performance.

3. Given two objects or sets, writes an appropriate order sentence. (writes order sentence)

4. Given an order sentence, validates it physically or pictorially. (validates order sentence)

5. Given an open order sentence, completes it. (completes open order sentence)

These objectives will appear in the report forms in abbreviated fashion. The content of the DMP contains suggested activities that relate to the objectives. The numbers of these activities also appear on the form (Figure 8.3).

	Objec-tives	1	2	3	4	5
Checklist		reads order sen-tence	chooses order sen-tence	writes order sen-tence	validates order sentence	completes open order sentence
Topic 2.9						
(Name)	Activ-ities	5–13	2, 11	3, 5–10 14	11–14	13, 14

Fig. 8.3 Example topic checklist form (DMP).

The report form in Figure 8.3, called the "Topic Checklist," is kept for the entire group of students working on the specific topic. Note that the activities that apply to the various objectives are listed by number. As the students successfully complete the activities, they can be "checked off" by indicating the numbers in the student's row.

The report form of Figure 8.4 is used for individual students. It covers five topics of the DMP, one of which is Topic 2.9.

The objectives for each topic are indicated, and checks and comments can be inserted as the student progresses through the objectives.

The form of Figure 8.5 consists of a group record card which covers several topics. The student names are listed across the top of the form and the objectives for each topic are briefly listed on the lefthand side. As students master the objectives, they can simply be checked.

The group record card is basically a summary of the individual progress card and the topic checklist. The group card does not contain diagnostic information but it does provide a picture of the state of the instruction for the topics covered. In this way, it provides valuable summary information for the entire group across several topics.

When the unit staff is focusing on individual students, the individual progress sheet is used. This report form would be the basis for any individual conferences with students. When the instruction of a single topic across the entire group is being considered, the data from the topic checklist would be used. Group performance across several topics would involve the data of the group record card. The actual forms are printed on different colored paper for easy identification.

Name _____

Individual Progress Sheet—Level 2

Topic	Objectives 1	2	3	4	5	Comments
2.7	reads comparison sentence	chooses comparison sentence	writes comparison sentence	validates comparison sentence	completes open comparison sentence	
2.8	compares and orders capacities	assigns capacity measurement				
2.9	reads order sentence	chooses order sentence	writes order sentence	validates order sentence	completes open order sentence	
2.10	moves in given direction	constructs path given points	chooses points			
2.11	states number for set 11–20	writes numeral 11–20	reads number 11–20	models number 11–20	orders numbers 0–20	

Fig. 8.4 Form for recording individual progress by topic (DMP).

Group Record Card
Level 2

student names

Topic	Objective		
2.1	1	describes shape	
	2	chooses region	
	3	states same or different	
2.2	1	compares two weights	
	2	orders two weights	
2.3	1	writes numeral 0–10	
2.4	1	orders several occurrences	
2.5	1	represents weight physically	
	2	assigns length measurement	
	3	assigns weight measurement	
	4	uses length measurements to compare and order	
	5	uses weight measurements to compare and order	
	6	uses numerousness measurements to compare and order	

Fig. 8.5 Example group record card form (DMP).

2.6	1	describes path	
	2	chooses path	
	3	constructs path	
2.7	1	reads comparison sentence	
	2	chooses comparison sentence	
	3	writes comparison sentence	
	4	validates comparison sentence	
	5	completes open comparison sentence	
2.8	1	compares and orders capacities	
	2	assigns capacity measurement	
2.9	1	reads order sentence	
	2	chooses order sentence	
	3	writes order sentence	
	4	validates order sentence	
	5	completes open order sentence	
2.10	1	moves in given direction	
	2	constructs path given points	
	3	chooses points	
2.11	1	states number for set 11–20	
	2	writes numeral 11–20	
	3	reads number 11–20	
	4	models number 11–20	
	5	orders numbers 0–20	

Fig. 8.5 Cont.

Recording Skill Performance—Reading Example

The *Wisconsin Design for Reading Skill Development* (1972) has several forms for summarizing data, including individual student folders, wall charts, and student profile cards. The example presented here will deal with interpretive reading skills since these kinds of skills are not assessed by pencil-and-paper tests.

The fact that skills such as those in interpretive reading are not assessed through formal test items does not make them any less important than those skills that are assessed by test items. It is equally important to develop a systematic approach to assessing student performance with respect to skills such as those of interpretive reading as for the Word Attack Skills, for example. The teacher should be knowledgeable of the kinds of student behaviors that are indicators of the skills.

The approach to observing students and recording information suggested here is one of several that could be used. It is taken from Otto and Chester (1976). Assuming the teachers know the kinds of student behaviors that are indicative of the skills, the number of times that the student will be observed during a given time (for example, three months) can be established. The frequency of occurrence of behaviors that are evidence of the skills can be recorded on a form such as that in Figure 8.6.

Name: Mary Smith   Grade: 2   Skill Area: Interpretive Reading

A.1 Reacts to pictures	A.1	9/6 (5)	12/6 (5)	
A.2 Story interest	A.2	9/8 (4)	12/6 (5)	
A.3 Mood of poems	A.3	9/15 (3)	11/12 (4)	
B.1 Sees humor	B.1	9/15 (3)	11/15 (4)	
B.2 Reads with expression	B.2	9/15 (2)	10/20 (3)	
B.3 Empathizes	B.3	9/12 (3)	11/6 (4)	
C.1 Character traits	C.1	9/15 (1)	10/22 (2)	
C.2 Story plots	C.2	9/12 (3)	11/17 (4)	
D.1 Motives of characters	D.1	9/12 (3)	11/17 (4)	
D.2 Story backgrounds	D.2	9/15 (2)	11/15 (3)	

Fig. 8.6 Example form for recording student performance relative to interpretive reading skills.

In the form of Figure 8.6 the student behaviors are keyed by letter and number to the objectives. The spaces provided are for the date of the observation and the numbers in parentheses the frequency of occurrence. The form can easily be placed on a 6″ × 8″ card. It is not likely that a teacher could systematically observe at a single occasion more behaviors than can be listed on a 6″ × 8″ card. A card is kept for each individual student.

Instead of recording the number of occurrences of a student behavior, a five-point scale consisting of never, seldom, occasionally, rather frequently, and very frequently can be used. The categories will need to be defined so that their meanings are consistent. Then for a given observation the appropriate category can be checked for each student behavior.

A record of the type described indicates the skills that the student is using regularly and satisfactorily. If skills are absent, it may be that the student is lacking the necessary prerequisites. Or the instructional situation may be such that there is little opportunity for the student to demonstrate the skills. Whatever the case, the record should be evidence of the situation.

All recording of teacher observation need not be done on record forms. It cannot always be anticipated when a student will engage in creative writing or divergent thinking, for example. If the student does demonstrate related behaviors, or if the student has difficulty in applying such skills, a note can be made when the observation occurs. Teachers can look for relevant behaviors related to one or two objectives on a daily basis. This type of observation is somewhat informal but it too can be recorded and provide useful assessment information.

USE OF ASSESSMENT INFORMATION WITHIN THE UNIT

Systematic record keeping will enhance the use of assessment information, especially the interpretation of such information. The interpretation of assessment information was introduced in Chapter 3 in connection with the planning of a test and comments on interpretation have been made throughout. Additional comments at this point are in order.

Basically, the communication of assessment information within the unit goes two ways: (1) among the members of the unit staff, especially the teachers, and (2) between teacher and student. Most interpretation occurs in the first case, although it should be clear to the student how the results of the student's performance are being interpreted.

Use of Assessment Information among Teachers

Students are interested primarily in the interpretation of results for themselves. Teachers, however, must interpret results for individual students, subgroups of students, and the entire group of students. Teachers are also concerned with the evaluation of overall instruction as well as whether instruction has been adequate for the individual student.

Communication among teachers about the integration of results takes place, for the most part, during unit staff meetings. At these meetings some time should be devoted specifically to interpreting information available on record forms. It is generally the unit leader who assumes the responsibility for leadership in interpreting results, but all teachers should actively participate.

The forms introduced earlier in this chapter should be very useful for communicating and interpreting results. Indeed, systematic record keeping is not an end in itself but a means to enhancing communication and interpretation.

Information on individual performance. Student performance must be interpreted on an individual basis. Although we often require full mastery as a criterion, this is not always the case. In fact, we have seen earlier that there are eight possible combinations of common or variable objectives, full mastery or variable criteria of attainment, and invariant or variable sequence of instructional units. Obviously, these combinations have implications for how assessment information is used.

The range of possibilities for these combinations is from most of the objectives being the same for many students to no objectives being the same for any two students. Many, but certainly not all, of the objectives in mathematics and reading are of the former type. Objectives of the latter type are more likely to occur in areas such as art or with special projects in science and social studies. Report forms that summarize performances of individual students (e.g., Fig. 8.2) are a necessity so that the information about a student can be interpreted in terms of the objectives that apply. That form also indicates whether or not the objective has been met regardless of the level of mastery specified in the criterion.

Suppose that in an area such as social studies the instructional units have a variable sequence. They need not be taken in the same order. (It is also possible that objectives *within* a unit have a variable sequence.) When communicating and interpreting assessment results, this condition must also be considered.

There is more to interpreting performance than simply indicating whether or not instructional objectives have been met. Suppose a student has not met certain objectives. Then the test items and work samples should be carefully examined in order to identify the student's deficiencies. Results of diagnostic item sets such as those discussed in Chapter 3 can be helpful. Supplemental information such as that provided by anecdotal records can be valuable in adequately describing the source of the deficiencies.

In most content and skills areas there is usually a variety of possible causes for not attaining objectives. Therefore, it is important to prescribe for each student the materials and procedures that would be most helpful in an attempt to meet the objectives not previously met. For these kinds of instructional decisions the information of the form in Figure 8.1 is helpful in that it indicates the actual performance level.

Suppose that several students have met a set of instructional objectives. In its simplest form for criterion-referenced assessment, this means that the students can begin work on the next instructional objectives in the sequence. For small bits of instruction this is the only interpretation that is necessary. However, whether the student has attained minimal criteria or some higher level of performance may have implications for future instruction. It may be that a high level of performance indicates "testing out" of some subsequent objectives. Or the level of performance may give some indication of the amount of time required for the next objectives in the sequence.

When summative testing and evaluation is taking place near the close of a relatively long instructional period, it may be necessary to distinguish among various levels of mastery for grading purposes. It is usually not adequate to simply grade by the dichotomy "mastery versus nonmastery" or "pass versus fail." Finer distinctions are usually required between levels of mastery and, conceptually at least, a student in an individualized program should not be failed. A student would not be assigned a grade until the criteria had been attained. Additional comments on reporting grades will be made in a following section.

Information on group performance. The information about group performance on a test, attaining objectives, etc., can be helpful in improving instruction. The patterns of group performance may indicate modifications of methods, reordering the sequence of objectives, or using different materials.

The report forms of Figures 8.3 and 8.5 provide summaries of group performance. Suppose that the students as a group are having difficulty meeting a subset of objectives. (The group would likely be a subgroup of the students in the unit, working on a common set of objectives at a given time.) What would be possible interpretations of the lack of attainment?

If the measurement for attaining the objectives consisted of one or more tests, the test items should be checked for ambiguity, poor construction, and the degree to which they reflect or relate to the objectives. The lack of attainment might be a function of inadequate measurement.

But, suppose that the test items appear to be adequate, what are other possible interpretations of the difficulty? Possibly the instruction has not been done well. IGE tends to guard against consistently poor instruction when either individuals or groups are considered, but it cannot eliminate all instances. Modifications in instructional methods might be indicated. Possibly the objectives are not sequenced properly for the level of this particular group.

When interpreting test results for either an individual or a group of students, it is important to consider subsets of items as they relate to specific objectives. For example, consider a test which would cover the five objectives listed in Figure 8.3 (Topic 2.9 of the DMP). Suppose a test contained 50 items and 80 percent correct was set as the criterion for satisfactory performance on the test. That means that a student could miss ten items and still meet the criterion.

If the objective "validates order sentence" was covered by eight items, it would be possible for a student to miss all eight items plus two others and still have the test performance considered satisfactory. But clearly the student is not meeting that particular objective. Therefore, it is seldom adequate, especially with longer tests, to rely on the interpretation of a total test score. The use of a form such as that of Figure 8.1 tends to guard against gross interpretation being incorrect for specific objectives. The interpretation must be made with respect to the instructional objectives.

The foregoing discussion illustrates that there are various ways of interpreting test and other performance results. There are basically two approaches, that of evaluating an individual's performance with respect to objectives attained, and that of evaluating the instructional program. Interpretations are often diagnostic in nature, and this is in keeping with instructional programming for the individual student. For specific content and curriculum programs, tests and other exercises are often provided with specific suggestions for the interpretation of results.

Use of Assessment Information between Teacher and Student

Every student should be kept apprised of progress in meeting the instructional objectives. It is not sufficient to report only test grades to students, and not relate them to the objectives. Results of student progress can be communicated to the student through a student-teacher conference. Many times communication does not require a formal conference, but every student should have occasions during the year when progress can be discussed with a teacher. Feedback to the student serves a guidance function and often a motivating function as well.

The goal-setting conferences of IGM (1973) have as part of their purposes transmitting information to the student. Certainly the primary initial purposes of the goal-setting conference are to increase a child's self-direction and motivation to learn, but these purposes cannot be met in an informational vacuum. Assessment information should be used in guiding the child to set realistic goals. Goal-setting conferences can be conducted on an individual basis or with small groups of children.

In a student-teacher conference information from forms such as those of Figures 8.1, 8.2, and 8.4 should be used. The student can be shown the progress toward meeting objectives. Interpretations should be made to the student. The student should have an opportunity to ask questions about the results and their interpretations. Reinforcement should be used to the extent possible, and information should be transmitted in a constructive manner.

The interpretation to a student of performance should be criterion-referenced. Rarely would a student be given norm-referenced interpretations. The status of other students in attaining the objectives should be of little concern to the student. For this reason, summary forms such as that of Figure 8.5 would not be used in a student-teacher conference.

When interpreting assessment results to a student the facts of performance should be discussed. However, the conference should not be a one-way conversation. If the student is not attaining the objectives anticipated, the student's opinion should also be considered. The teacher can use questions such as:

Do you think the objectives were not right for you?

Are there some things outside of school interfering with your school-work?

Do you think that if you studied with other students it would be helpful?

Of course, the student should be reinforced for the objectives attained. Strong points in the student's performance should be praised. The conference should not only be informative for the student, but should also be motivational.

USE OF ASSESSMENT INFORMATION AT THE SCHOOL LEVEL

Historically, the use of assessment information within a school or entire system has been for summative evaluation, usually toward the close of the school year. Most of these evaluations have been comprehensive with respect to content and their interpretations have been primarily norm-referenced. In some cases schools and classes are positioned with respect to national norms and local norms for the system.

School and systemwide summative evaluations still persist in some instances and in many cases for good reason. But in an IGE school, evaluation at the school level should be largely formative. It should be conducted during the school year while instruction is taking place with the expressed aim of improving the instructional programs and enhancing student learning.

An I & R Unit's formal link with the IIC is the unit leader who is a member of the IIC. As information from the unit is required by the IIC, it is the unit leader's responsibility to provide for obtaining the information. Since the instructional objectives are built upon the broader educational objectives, group progress toward meeting instructional objectives is the major source of information for evaluating the attainment of educational objectives.

If school- or system-level summative evaluations are conducted, there is usually little question about the forms used for reporting student progress. Usually some kind of standardized, published test is used and the forms accompany the tests. When the IIC is obtaining information to be used in their formative evaluations during the year, they can develop reporting forms which summarize information across relatively large numbers of students.

REPORTING TO PARENTS—WRITTEN

If the majority of the assessment for instructional programming for the individual student is criterion-referenced, it would logically follow that grading systems should be criterion-referenced and the subsequent reporting to parents would be based on criterion-referenced interpretations of a student's performance. Historically, marks were criterion-referenced, at least in a technical sense, since criteria such as 94 percent or better performance earned an A, etc. However, over the past several decades, the interpretation of marks has tended to be heavily norm-referenced, and many parents have a strong orientation toward this type of interpretation.

Parents' Frame of Reference for Student Progress

When a parent is perusing a report card, or discussing a student's performance with a teacher, the basic questions of the parent are, "Is the performance satisfactory?" or "How is my child doing?" What the parent is asking is whether or not the child is making satisfactory progress and usually the only frame of reference that the parent has is the progress of other students. To some extent this causes a reporting dilemma for the teacher when instruction is programmed for the individual student.

The dilemma does not stem from the inability to put the results, even if they come from criterion-referenced tests, into a norm-referenced frame. This could be easily done by positioning student performance with respect to the performances of peers or available norms. The dilemma arises from an inconsistency between using norm-referenced interpretations when the purpose of the instruction clearly requires criterion-referenced interpretation.

Although the dilemma exists, it can be at least partially overcome by emphasizing what the student can do. It is not easy to do this without referring to the performance of other students. However, there are scores that can be used with criterion-referenced assessment. Not all of these kinds of scores are necessarily reported to parents, but they can be used as an information base in describing a student's performance.

Scores for Criterion-referenced Assessment

The characteristic that distinguishes criterion-referenced from norm-referenced interpretation is its emphasis on describing the absolute rather than the relative level of performance with respect to an objective or skill. This necessitates kinds of scores or information different from the usual relative positioning scores, such as percentiles, associated with norm-referenced assessment. Examples of different kinds of scores that have been suggested are as follows:

1. The number or percent correct on a given objective or set of items that encompass a few highly related objectives.
2. "Mastery" of a given objective or set of items where "mastery" is defined in terms of a certain level of performance such as 90 percent correct.
3. The time it takes (such as in class hours or calendar days) for an individual to achieve a given performance level (including what has been defined as "mastery"). (Harris 1973)
4. The time (in minutes or hours) it takes a student to perform a

certain task or set of tasks related to an objective (such as correctly computing the product of all single digit numerals).

5. The probability that the student is ready to begin the next level of instruction (this may be based on both the number of items correct and the pattern of answers given to these items).

6. The percentage of students who "pass" each item; that is, the item's difficulty. This kind of score is used exclusively in program evaluation where each item or task is considered important in itself. (Klein and Kosecoff 1973, pp. 8–9)

The kinds of scores receiving the most attention indicate whether or not the student has attained mastery. There are two basic difficulties with the use of mastery scores. One is that in most cases the definition of "mastery" is quite arbitrary. There are numerous criteria that are used such as "80 percent correct," or "85 percent correct," on a test or exercise. Usually, the items are samplings or reflections of the skills and content to be mastered, and the establishment of the criterion is quite subjective.

The second difficulty which is usually of more concern to parents is that the dichotomy mastery versus nonmastery obscures the true level of student performance. It simply is not informative enough. If a student has attained mastery, did the student just make it, or did the student come in considerably above the minimum level for mastery? If a student has not attained mastery, did the performance just miss or was it a long way off? Therefore, instead of focusing attention on mastery it is well to focus on the progress the student is making toward attaining objectives.

There are a number of ways that written reports, typically called report cards, to parents can be structured. Some schools are required, for whatever reasons, to persist with traditional letter grades on report cards. In any event the report card should be structured so that it provides a maximum summary of information about the student's performance, attitude, etc., and yet remains within reasonable length. Examples of possible approaches are now considered.

Relating Mastery to Letter Grades

The assignment of letter grades over the years, regardless of some people's impression, has been subjective. Somewhere in the process someone, usually a teacher, sets arbitrary standards. Basically, what has occurred is that knowingly or unknowingly students and parents rely on the professional judgment of the teacher.

With attainment of objectives in a criterion-referenced framework the situation is not much different. Gronlund (1973, p. 44) suggests one approach to assigning letter grades that takes into account the student's performance on "developmental" objectives. These are objectives that measure student development beyond the minimum, mastery level. They are instructional objectives. Gronlund's suggestions are:

A—achieved all mastery objectives and high on developmental objectives.

B—achieved all mastery objectives and low on developmental objectives.

C—achieved all mastery objectives only.

D or E—nonmastery.

At least theoretically, students would not be failed. They would simply not be assigned a letter grade until they had met the criteria of the objectives. Practically, because of time constraints and other reasons, the required delay may not be possible and grades such as D, E, or F are used.

The matter of mastery versus nonmastery as a dichotomy is not the most frequently used procedure for evaluation when programming instruction for the individual student. In practice it is used sparingly. For the majority of instructional objectives, student performance is evaluated in terms of progress and achievement appropriate for the specific student. In some cases a change of direction is the criterion for evaluating student behavior. This might occur, for example, in attempting to change undesirable work habits of a student.

The concepts of student progress and achievement appropriate for the specific student are reflected in the markings of the example report cards discussed in the next section. Nowhere on those report cards do the words mastery or nonmastery appear. The descriptors are designed to convey more meaning than that contained in a simple dichotomy.

Descriptors of Pupil Performance

One goal of the written report card is to describe pupil performance accurately and succinctly in a way that is meaningful to the parents. There are any number of ways by which this can be done. Usually, gross descriptors over entire content and skills areas are not adequate. Examples of such gross descriptors would be "superior in mathematics" or "at grade level in reading." On the other hand, it is not feasible to provide the parent with the detailed breakdown of objectives, tests, etc., that the teachers use for internal record keeping.

Reports to parents must communicate accurately.

Examples of report cards that contain descriptors of pupil performance are found in the following figures.* These examples contain check marks or indicators, but do not use letter grades. Note that the descriptors are not limited to cognitive performance. Affective characteristics are also included. In the example of Figure 8.7 (Glendale Elementary School, Toledo, Ohio) there are descriptors dealing with social adjustment.

---

* These examples have been used in IGE schools and have been found to be effective. It should be remembered that the parent-teacher conference is an important part of home-school communication and supplements the written report.

Pupil_____ Year 19____ 19____

	1	2	3	4	Total
Days Absent					
Times Tardy					

1 and 3 Quarters <u>CONFERENCES</u> <u>ONLY</u>

MARKING: The marks below show your child's progress.

Each achievement level is checked when your child shows evidence of understanding.

Achieving satisfactorily	✓
Class Average	*
Below expectation; needs to improve	–
Superior Achievement	★

The ✓ indicates your child's own achievement; the asterisk * indicates the class average; the – minus sign indicates areas to be worked on. Only those areas taught during the grading period are marked.

LANGUAGE ARTS

READING LEVEL:

    Extended readiness

    Reading readiness

    Pre-Primer

    Primer

    First Reader

    2nd Reader - 1st level

    2nd Reader - 2nd level

    Above second year level

    Supplementary Enrichment

READING:

    Reads silently with understanding

    Shows vocabulary growth

    Uses phonetic skills

    Uses structural analysis skills

    Uses other word attack skills

    Reads well orally

    Reads independently

ORAL AND WRITTEN COMMUNICATION:

    Speaks distinctly and audibly

    Uses good vocabulary, full sentences

    Listens, contributes to discussions

    Listens to directions affectively

    Uses correct oral and written grammar

    Capitalizes correctly in writing

    Expresses original ideas in writing

HANDWRITING:

    Uses correct form and spacing

    Prepares papers neatly in all work

    Legible form used in all written work

SPELLING: 1 2 3 4
   Is able to spell needed words
   Retains and correctly uses words taught   75

MATH:
   Recognizes sets through ten
   Understands cardinal idea of numbers (greater, less, equal to)
   Understands ordinals (first, second)
   Understands preparation for facts
   Knows basic facts: addition
                      subtraction
                      multiplication
                      division
   Understands problem-solving: formation of equations
   Understands measurement
   Understands place value
   Counts: ones, fives, tens, twenty-five
   Recognizes denominations of money   75
   Knows how to make change

SCIENCE:
   Shows questioning attitude
   Seeks explanations of natural phenomenon

WORK HABITS:
   Makes good use of work periods
   Completes work in adequate time
   Works accurately and carefully
   Follows directions independently
   Is responsible for work, materials
   Uses basic reference materials
   Responds positively to school work, shows interest and confidence

SOCIAL STUDIES AND SOCIAL ADJUSTMENT:
   Works and plays well with others
   Respects rights, property of others
   Practices good manners, safety rules
   Shows self-control
   Profits by constructive criticism
   Respects authority
   Awareness of the interdependence of community workers
   Knowledge of local community (neighborhood resources)

Your child's assignment for next year is:

Respectfully, _____ , Teacher

Fig. 8.7 Example report card including indicators of social adjustment.

What records can the I & R Unit staff use when completing the affective portion of a report card? One approach, probably the least desirable, is to rely on memory at the time the report card is completed. A more effective approach is to review notes or anecdotal records taken on the student during the grading period.

The record keeping on affective characteristics or objectives can be extended further. Report forms similar to those of the interpretive reading skills example discussed earlier in the chapter can be developed. The descriptors of affective performance, for example, "works and plays well with others," can be exactly the same as in the report card (see the lower, righthand portion of Figure 8.7). The student can then be periodically observed and rated on an appropriate scale such as "never" to "always." (The scale, of course, must fit the descriptor of affective performance.)

The report card of Figure 8.7 also contains a section on work habits. The student can be systematically observed on the work habits and behaviors listed as well. These kinds of behaviors are evidenced (or not) in the day-to-day instruction and the teachers should be aware of whether or not the student is demonstrating them adequately.

There is an option for a norm-referenced interpretation in the report card. Note that achievement can be marked as "class average." However, other markings are reserved for criterion-referenced interpretations. The report form of Figure 8.8 was designed specifically for IGE schools as indicated in the title. The form is appropriate for the primary level. An interesting characteristic of this report card is that it contains both norm-referenced and criterion-referenced interpretations of the student's performance. The norm-referenced interpretation comes in sparingly, appearing only for language arts and mathematics. The norm-referenced interpretation appears in the far left column and grade level is used as the normative score.

The criterion-referenced interpretations, which appear in the right-hand columns of a section, contain much more detail than the norm-referenced interpretations. This particular report card has the option of having performance in the subject areas taught by the unit staff, marked by up to four teachers. This option provides additional information for the parents by indicating the consistency or lack of consistency in marking across teachers. Most I & R Unit staffs reach a consensus among themselves and provide a single grade.

The areas of art, music, and physical education are listed singly and very briefly on the report form. Note that in this section of the report card attitudes are marked. In these areas the estimate of a student's level of interest and, to a large extent, performance is primarily a subjective judgment made by the teacher. Nevertheless, there are student behaviors that can be observed and recorded that are indicators of student interest and attitude.

The report form also contains a section on social attitudes. The descriptors in this section are straightforward and reflect definite student behaviors that can be observed.

A very desirable feature of the report form of Figure 8.8 is the section for teacher comments. There is also the option for the parents to request a conference. This option should exist at any time in an IGE school. However, putting in a written reminder may motivate some conferences that would otherwise not take place.

The report cards of both Figures 8.7 and 8.8 are appropriate for the primary level. The report card of Figure 8.7 contains a greater array of specific behaviors, especially in mathematics and reading, than the report card of Figure 8.8. The latter report card contains the

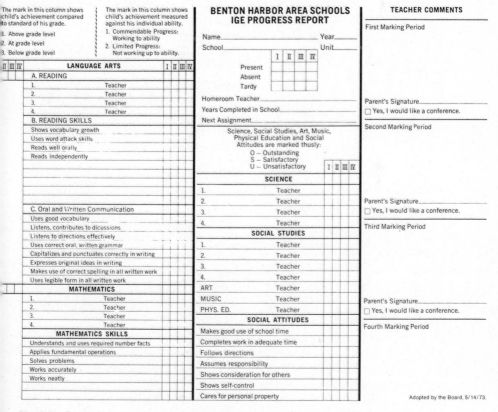

Fig. 8.8 Example progress report form designed specifically for IGE schools.

space for teacher comments and also includes art, music, and physical education separately. Both report forms include indicators of attitudes or social adjustment, a very important feature. The cards are very good illustrations of written report cards. They contain much information on a single page.

The report forms of Figures 8.9 and 8.10 are used in the same school system (Eau Claire, Wisconsin). The first form is used for the kindergarten level and the latter for the intermediate level. Although the reports have the same general form, the content and descriptors differ and are appropriate for the grade level. Note that social development, habits, and attitudes are included. The report is also coordinated with the parent-teacher conferences that are conducted during the year. These, too, are very good examples of report cards.

Report cards must be structured so that it is efficient for the teachers to complete them. Extensive narratives should be avoided,

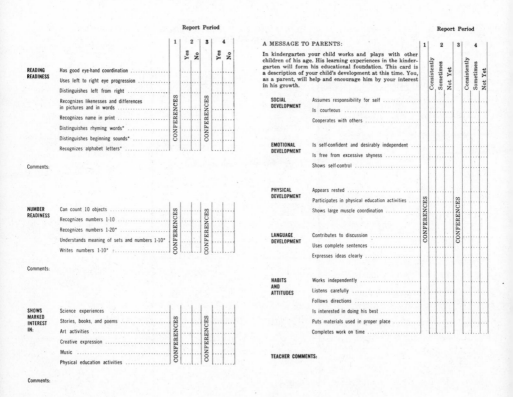

Fig. 8.9 Example report card used for the kindergarten level.

EXPLANATION OF MARKS

S - Satisfactory progress: progress is satisfactory
    according to this pupil's ability

N - Needs to improve: progress is not satisfactory
    according to this pupil's ability

Your child's teacher has used observation of classwork
and teacher-made tests as the basis for these marks. If
you wish to have more information, please make arrangements to talk with the teacher.

EXPLANATION OF MARKS

A check (✓) indicates that the behavior described is
often shown by your child. Content of the items checked is
as important as the number of items check. Please read
all items, as the unchecked ones also provide information
about your child.

Fig. 8.10 Example report card used for the intermediate level.

although brief, anecdotal comments may be appropriate. In an IGE
school, the completion of the report cards is a task for the unit staff.
All teachers with relevant input should have the opportunity to be
involved in the completion of the report for a specific child.

One of the components of IGE is the program of home-school
communications and that component is impossible to attain simply
through written reports. Therefore, an important part of this component is the parent-teacher conference which, among other things, involves a verbal report to the parent of pupil performance.

REPORTING TO PARENTS—VERBAL

The parent-teacher conference is usually conducted between a teacher
and one or both of the parents. Only by special request or under
atypical circumstances would the parents meet with all teachers of a

unit. In an IGE school it is usually the IIC that does the routine planning for scheduling the conferences.

We discussed earlier the parents' frame of reference and the dilemma that this norm-referenced frame might cause. If report cards have been distributed prior to the conference or if the parents are familiar with the kinds of report cards used, they may be somewhat in tune with criterion-referenced assessment. In any event, it is important that the teacher explain the emphasis of instructional programming for the individual student so that the parents are clear as to the basis on which performance is being discussed.

The teacher should briefly review the student's records prior to the conference so that comments and responses to questions are based on information in the records. It is important that the teacher be consistent between comments in the conference and what appears on the report card if a report has gone out or will go out shortly.

The teacher should be prepared to explain the use of instructional objectives and elaborate on the meaning of the various descriptors of pupil performance that are used, especially those on the report card. The usual guidelines for effectively conducting parent-teacher conferences apply. These have been summarized by Romano (1948) as:

1. Establish a friendly atmosphere free from interruption.
2. Be positive—begin and end the conference by enumerating favorable points.
3. Be truthful, yet tactful.
4. Be constructive in all suggestions to pupils and parents.
5. Help parents to achieve better understanding of their child as an individual.
6. Respect parents' and children's information as confidential.
7. Remain poised throughout the conference.
8. Be a good listener; let parents talk.
9. Observe professional ethics at all times.
10. Help parents find their own solutions to a problem.
11. Keep vocabulary simple; explain new terminology.
12. If notes are taken during the conference, review them with parents.
13. Invite parents to visit and participate in school functions.
14. Base your judgments on all available facts and on actual situations.
15. Offer more than one possible solution to a problem.

SUMMARY

The emphasis of this final chapter has been on the systematic record keeping and reporting to parents that enhances instructional programming for the individual student. The various forms that are used are not ends in themselves but means by which the evaluation system supports the instruction.

The forms used within the unit are generally of two types, those for individual students and those for summarizing across groups of students. Since instruction is based on instructional objectives, performance records must be related to such objectives. With the emphasis on the individual, individual records of performance must be kept. Summary forms across students are also necessary for the efficient management of information. Examples of forms that have been used effectively have been provided in this chapter.

Reporting pupil progress to parents is the responsibility of the teachers. Both written and verbal reporting are used when individualizing instruction and report cards involve more than the traditional letter grade forms. Indeed, letter grades are not necessary nor particularly desirable. Examples of report card forms and descriptors of pupil progress have been presented.

Evaluation is a very important part of the instructional process when programming instruction for the individual student. It is not an adjunct to instruction, considered only at various points for summative purposes. The day-to-day operation of the unit requires that evaluation and its related activities be a continuous part of instruction.

DISCUSSION TOPICS

1. Contrast the kinds of information on pupil progress found in forms for individual students and those for groups of students.

2. Describe the information that would be common to conferences between teachers and conferences between a student and a teacher. What types of information would be discussed between a student and a teacher but would not be considered in a unit staff meeting?

3. Describe the dilemma that can occur due to the differences in the kinds of pupil performance information the teacher has, and the kind parents are expecting. Discuss ways around the dilemma. Why do you think the parent-teacher conference is an important, really an essential part of the home-school communications in an IGE school.

REFERENCES

Developing mathematical processes, sampler 2. Madison, Wisc.: Wisconsin Research and Development Center for Cognitive Learning.

Gronlund, N. E. 1973. *Preparing criterion-referenced tests for classroom instruction.* New York: Macmillan.

Harris, C. W. 1973. Comments on problems of objectives-based measurement. Paper presented at the annual AERA meeting, New Orleans.

Klausmeier, H. J., *et al.* 1973. *Individually guided motivation.* Madison, Wisc.: Wisconsin Research and Development Center for Cognitive Learning.

Klein, S. P., and J. Kosecoff 1973. Issues and procedures in the development of criterion-referenced tests. *TM Report 26.* Princeton: ERIC Clearinghouse on Tests, Measurement, and Evaluation.

Romano, L. 1949. The parent-teacher conference, *NEA Journal* 48:21–22.

Wisconsin Design for Reading Skill Development 1972. Madison, Wisc.: The University of Wisconsin.

Appendix

The Construction of Test Items

The main content of this text emphasizes evaluation procedures, and there is no specific discussion on the construction of test items. When programming instruction for the individual student, teachers frequently use published tests or test items that accompany published curriculum materials. Nevertheless, there is always a need at some time for teachers to construct their own items. This appendix deals with the technical aspects of constructing test items in some of the more commonly used formats.

Although an item is neither criterion-referenced or norm-referenced until the results on the test of which it is a part are interpreted, items of the objective type are used predominantly with criterion-referenced testing. A variety of formats can be used for objective items and they are discussed in this appendix.

Essay items require a longer response than objective items, and there is usually some subjectivity in scoring the response. Essay items are used sparingly in the elementary school, especially at the lower levels. However, there may be occasion for using essay items when programming instruction for the individual student.

OBJECTIVE ITEMS

The kinds of items that are commonly used in paper-and-pencil tests for assessing achievement in cognitive areas can be dichotomized into two broad types, objective and essay items. Objective items are those that require the student to supply a short answer or to select an answer from two or more options. Basically, the definition of objectivity in test items is contained in the scoring: "... the extent to which equally competent scorers get the same results." Items that require short responses tend to lend themselves more to objectivity in the scoring and for that reason the term objective item is used.

Types of Item Formats

There are four commonly used item formats for objective items, and these are (1) true-false, (2) multiple-choice, (3) matching, and (4) short answer. The true-false item is one in which the student is provided with a statement and indicates whether the statement is true or false. A multiple-choice item is an item that presents a statement (called the stem) and the student is required to select one of two or more (usually more) options that correctly completes the statement or correctly answers the problem posed in the statement. The traditional format of the matching item contains two columns, one consisting of questions or statements, and a second column consisting of correct "matches" or associations with the statements of the first column. The student is required to associate or "match" the statements of the two columns. There must be at least two entries in each column, but usually there are many more. The short answer item may consist of a statement with a word or phrase missing (filling in the blank) or the item may be a question which requires an answer of one word or very few words.

Advantages and Disadvantages of Objective Items

Objective test items have some definite advantages. One advantage is that they are efficient in terms of student time. It takes a relatively short time for a student to respond to an item. For this reason, many more objective items than essay items can be presented in a given time and therefore the instructional content can be more extensively and adequately sampled. This, of course, results in higher content validity for the test. If traditional, norm-referenced approaches to reliability are used, the increased number of items in the test also tends to increase the test reliability.

The scoring of objective items requires much less time than the scoring of essay items. With its objectivity, objective items can be accurately scored with little if any dispute about the correctness of response. In general, objective items provide an efficient means by which performance information can be obtained from students.

The major disadvantage of objective type items usually cited is that they fail to measure higher mental processes, those required by learning outcomes in the higher levels of the taxonomy. These outcomes include those in classifications such as synthesis and evaluation. Many authors would argue against this criticism.* The position in this text is that objective items can be constructed to measure higher levels of mental performance. However, there would be no great value in excluding the use of essay items in IGE and therefore it is recommended that both types be used as appropriate.

One disadvantage sometimes attributed to objective items is the time required in their construction. Considering this a disadvantage arises partly from the misconception that essay items are easy to construct, that practically any questions will do. Generally, it does take less time to construct an essay test than an objective test, but this is because many fewer items are required for the essay test.

---

* See, for example, W. Mehrens and I. Lehmann 1973. *Measurement and evaluation in education and psychology*. New York: Holt, Rinehart and Winston.

General Principles of Constructing Items

There are generally accepted principles or rules for preparing objective test items regardless of the item format and many of these also apply to the preparation of essay items. If the test is criterion-referenced and even if it is norm-referenced, it is important that the test items require the specific behaviors or a sampling thereof that are contained in the instructional objectives. The behaviors listed with each objective while planning the test provide the basis for the behaviors included in the items.

Items should be definitive and written in clear, concise language. The language should be appropriate for the student's level, and the terminology should be familiar to the student. Irrelevant or nonfunctional content in an item should be avoided. Such content may distract the student from the important content of the item, or even prevent the student from responding correctly. For example, students should not be prevented from responding correctly to the items of a science test because the reading level required of the items is beyond their reading levels.

Test items should not provide clues to answers of other items in the test. For example, with multiple-choice items the stem of one item may contain the answer or a partial answer to another item. There are other ways that clues to answers can be given inadvertently such as grammatical inconsistencies. The correct response may be so different from the distractors in a multiple-choice item that it can be selected on this basis alone. Sometimes students can eliminate optional responses due to such extraneous factors. If incorrect grammar is used with the correct response, this may be confusing to the student and cause a wrong response.

Consider the following item:

Which of the following is not a city on the Eastern Seaboard:

A. Montana

B. New York

C. Boston

D. Norfolk

The student could respond correctly to this item by knowing that Montana is not a city. The item basically fails to measure the student's knowledge of cities on the Eastern Seaboard. The item also has another weakness in that it is negatively stated. The negative aspect is sometimes confusing to students. Depending on the objectives, a negatively stated item may miss the desired learning outcome. Knowing what is not on the Eastern Seaboard does not necessarily indicate that the student knows what is.

Grammatical inconsistencies most commonly appear in the use of the articles "a" and "an" and in the tense of the verbs. Multiple-choice items are especially susceptible to grammatical inconsistencies, partly because of the need for distractors. Consider the following item:

> The analysis of rocks brought back from the moon can be used:
>
> A. locating landing sites
>
> B. in determining the age of the moon
>
> C. they provide comparisons with earth rocks
>
> D. electroanalyses

Responses A, C, and D do not fit with the stem of the item. Even if the student considers these responses as possibly being correct, the incorrect grammar causes confusion.

Thus far we have considered general principles for preparing objective items. Since additional comments are relevant to specific item formats, they will now be discussed individually.

True-False Items

A true-false item is one in which the student is provided with a statement and is to indicate whether the statement is true or false. True-false items are best used in situations in which there are only two alternatives. If more than two alternatives exist it is usually better to use another item format.

True-false items have the disadvantage of false statements being responded to correctly on the basis of misinformation, or in the absence of knowing the correct answer. Consider the item:

> T   F   The product of 1/3 and 3/4 is 4/7.

A student may respond by marking F, which is the correct response, and not know the correct product. The student may think that the correct product is 3/7, for example. A student could be making serious errors in the multiplication of fractions, and still respond correctly to this item.

The true-false item is not useful for diagnostic purposes. If a student responds incorrectly it is not possible to analyze the incorrect option selected, as with a multiple-choice item, or the actual response as in a short-answer item.

When true-false items are used, they should be limited to two alternative situations. The statement of the item should be either true or false, not partially true. Negative statements should be minimized to the extent possible and certainly complicated wording and the use of the double negative should be avoided.

Any kind of structural "giveaway" in the statements should be checked and eliminated. For example, such a giveaway might be that the false statements are always considerably longer than true statements. Qualifiers such as always, never, and about, should be avoided. For example, the item, "The product of 1/3 and 3/4 is about 1/4," is a poor false item. The teacher might reason that the product is exactly 1/4, not about 1/4. A student could very well know the correct product, but respond incorrectly to the item.

If a test consists entirely of true-false items, the numbers of true and false statements should be approximately equal. This characteristic reduces the likelihood of correct guessing. The pattern of true and false statements should be random. This avoids a correct response pattern that may be discovered by the student.

Multiple-choice Items

The multiple-choice item is the most popular of the objective items. The item format is widely adaptable to content, skills, and objectives. Items of this format can be used to assess learning outcomes over the entire span of the taxonomy for instructional objectives, although it could be argued that they are most useful for measuring outcomes through the application level.

Forms for presenting the stem. It has already been mentioned that one part of the multiple-choice item is the stem; the part which presents a statement or problem. The other part consists of the options or alternatives, at least one of which is a correct (or best) response. Options which are incorrect are called distractors or foils. The stem of the item can be stated as a question or as an incomplete statement. In the former, the options consist of possible answers to the question, in the latter, the options provide completions of the statement.

There appears to be little empirical evidence as to the better method for presenting the stem of a multiple-choice item. The question form reduces the likelihood of grammatical inconsistencies, but it tends to require longer statements as options. The question form may be easier to structure and places less demand on reading skills, in order to be understood. For this reason, the question form may be preferable with younger children.

Variations of the multiple-choice item. There are numerous variations of the multiple-choice item but the four most commonly used are (1) one correct answer, (2) best answer, (3) analogy type, and (4) reverse type. Of these variations, the first two are most commonly used for teacher prepared tests. The analogy type is more commonly found on published aptitude, achievement, or attitude inventories than on teacher prepared tests. The reverse type is not commonly used on teacher-prepared tests.

The first two variations listed are exactly what the name implies; there is one correct or best answer and the student is to select one and only one option. The items of Figure A.1 illustrate the one correct answer and the best answer type. These items deal with the study skills of locating information. Item No. 2 would likely have a single correct response, namely D. On the other hand, information relative to Item No. 3 could likely be found in C, D, and E; however, D is the best response.

The analogy type item also requires the student to select one and only one option. A relationship is indicated between two concepts or things; the student is required to deduce this relationship and apply it to two other concepts or things, one of which is given and the other appears as one of the options. An example of an analogy type item is:

California is to Sacramento as New York is to:

A. Syracuse

B. Rochester

C. Buffalo

D. Albany

The correct response is, of course, based on the relationship of a state to its capital.

The reverse type item has all but one of the options correct. Although not widely used in teacher-prepared tests, it works well in situations for which it is difficult to construct distractors, but several facts or characteristics are true about the concept in the stem. Reverse type multiple-choice items can be confusing to the student because attention is focused on an incorrect rather than correct response. Usually the student is directed to select the incorrect option. An example of a reverse type item is:

Directions: Select the response which is not correct.

Identify the forms of transportation considered to be public transportation:

A. commuter train

B. bus

C. automobile

D. airplane shuttle

D.11.b
Form I

Test 22
Headings and Subheadings

Use the reference page below to answer questions X and Y.

EXAMPLES

X.   What mountains are in California?

○ read part A   ○ read part E
○ read part B   ○ read part F
○ read part C   ○ read every part
○ read part D

Y.   Where was the first capital of California?

○ read part A   ○ read part E
○ read part B   ○ read part F
○ read part C   ○ read every part
○ read part D

Use the reference page below to answer questions 1-4.

1.   What are the major food crops grown in Oregon?

○ read part A   ○ read part E
○ read part B   ○ read part F
○ read part C   ○ read every part
○ read part D

2.   What was the route of the Oregon Trail?

○ read part A   ○ read part E
○ read part B   ○ read part F
○ read part C   ○ read every part
○ read part D

3.   How did the settlers live?

○ read part A   ○ read part E
○ read part B   ○ read part F
○ read part C   ○ read every part
○ read part D

4.   What city is the capital of Oregon?

○ read part A   ○ read part E
○ read part B   ○ read part F
○ read part C   ○ read every part
○ read part D

GO ON TO THE NEXT PAGE

Fig. A.1   Example items having one correct answer or a best answer.

With the directions as given, the correct response is C. Whenever reverse type items are used, special precautions in directions must be taken to ensure that the student knows what is expected.

When constructing multiple-choice items there may be an inclination to use "all of the above" as the final option. Actually, this option is seldom if ever recommended. For one thing, a student who identifies just one other option as being incorrect can eliminate "all of the above" as the correct response. On the other hand, if a minimum of two other options are identified as correct, then "all of the above" is obviously the correct response. This condition can be countered by using combinations of responses as options such as "A and B" or "A and C but not D." However, using combinations of responses tends to make for more complicated and difficult items that may be confusing, especially to younger students.

The option "none of the above" can be used as a correct response or useful distractor when an absolute standard of correctness is involved. An arithmetic item might be an example. However, this option should be used sparingly. A student may respond correctly simply because none of the other options is recognized as correct. Adding this option to an item tends to reduce, certainly not eliminate, the effect of guessing.

Developing distractors. One of the most difficult tasks of preparing multiple-choice items is developing "good" distractors. Without good distractors the student may be able to arrive at the correct response through a process of elimination, rather than through actually knowing the correct response. Distractors should be of such a nature that they are arrived at through the use of misinformation or an error in reasoning. Consider the concept used earlier in a true-false item, put into a multiple-choice format:

The product of 1/3 and 3/4 is:

A. 3/7

B. 1/4

C. 1/3

D. 4/7

The three distractors can each be arrived at through an error in mathematical operations. It would not be desirable to have as distractors 5, 10.834, or 5/19, for example. Nor would it be desirable to put B, the correct response in decimal form (.25) and leave the distractors in fraction form. The purpose of this item is not to test for skill in converting fractions to decimals, but, if it were, all options should be presented as decimals. Characterizing the correct option in a way that is not parallel with the distractors should be avoided. Even the length of the options should be somewhat consistent. The options should also be parallel in content. For example, in phrasing an item about Civil War personalities, include only individuals that lived during that period.

Inadvertent clues to the correct option. There are any number of ways that clues to the correct option can be inadvertently included in a multiple-choice item. Grammatical clues, lack of parallel options, and a distinguishing length to the correct option have already been mentioned. The wording of the stem may also provide a clue to the correct option, especially if a word or a variation of a word in the stem also appears in the correct option. Consider the following item.

The instrument used to remove humidity from the air is the:

A. Barometer
B. Thermometer
C. Dehumidifier
D. Hygrometer

The clue in the stem, of course, is the "humidity" to go with the option, dehumidifier. A synonym for humidity should be used in the stem if the item is to be retained in its present form. Content clues can also be obtained from other items if items are overlapping in information.

When considering true-false items, it was mentioned that no definite pattern of true and false statements should appear. By the same token, when using multiple-choice items the correct response should not consistently appear in a given position or pattern. All positions should appear with approximately equal frequency, but this does not eliminate the possibility of a pattern of correct responses appearing. The correct positions should be randomly assigned to the items of the test. Another way to eliminate a pattern of correct response is to alphabetize the options.

Number of options. There is no definite number of options that must be included in a multiple-choice item. Four or five options appear to be the most frequently used numbers. Although test reliability tends to increase with increased numbers of options, there are practical matters to consider. Obtaining greater numbers of adequate distractors becomes increasingly difficult. This depends to some extent upon the nature of the material covered in the test, but for some content it is practically impossible to come up with more than three or four plausible distractors. The comprehension level (usually associated with age) of the students must also be considered. Since the student must comprehend the entire item, items with fewer options are usually used with lower comprehension level students. For this reason two or three option items are frequently used with children in primary level units. However, a word of caution on using small numbers of options. Evidence provided by Niedermeyer and Sullivan* indicated that three-option items do not discriminate between good and poor readers at the primary level, whereas four-option items do. It is not necessary that all the multiple-choice items of a test have the same number of options although many times this is the case.

The multiple-choice item is versatile and can be used with pictures, maps, and diagrams as well as with items consisting of words only. Examples of items used in this way appear in Figures A.2 and A.3. In order to measure higher level learning outcomes—such as analysis—unusual, creative organization, of content of the item may be required. Nevertheless, the multiple-choice item is well suited for measuring learning outcomes beyond simple knowledge level. The items should be carefully worded following the suggestions presented earlier. After items are initially developed, they should be reviewed and revised as necessary.

Matching Items

The matching item commonly appears in a two-column format, although variations on this format can be used. The two columns of a matching item are commonly called the premises and responses. Matching items lend themselves well to testing a knowledge of relationships or definitions.

One advantage that a matching item has over a multiple-choice item is that it does not require the construction of plausible distractors. However, the correct response for any premise should also serve as a plausible response for the other premises. Thus, although the large numbers of plausible distractors are not required, it does take skill and time to construct good matching items with plausible responses. The matching item does provide the opportunity to compress a considerable amount of content or questions into a single item which requires a relatively small amount of testing time. In this way content sampling and content validity tend to be enhanced.

Constructing the matching item. A matching item should deal with homogeneous content, usually a single concept or a single basis for classification. For example, we would not construct a matching item which contains historical events and book titles in one column and dates and authors in the second column. If these classifications were

---

*   F. C. Niedermeyer and H. J. Sullivan 1972. Differential effects of individual and group testing strategies in an objectives-based instructional program. *J. Educational Measurement* 9:199–204.

Test 4
Scale: Fractional Units

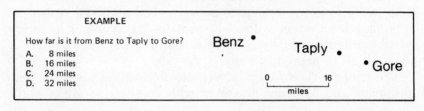

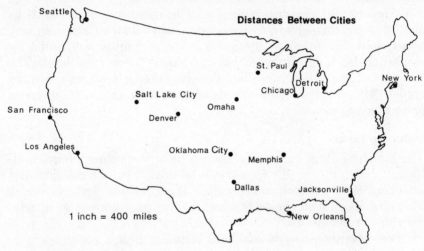

Distances Between Cities

1 inch = 400 miles

1. How far is it from Chicago to Omaha to San Francisco?
   - A.   1200 miles
   - B.   1300 miles
   - C.   1600 miles
   - D.   1700 miles
   - E.   1800 miles

2. How far is it from Jacksonville to New York to Detroit?
   - A.   800 miles
   - B.   1000 miles
   - C.   1200 miles
   - D.   1300 miles
   - E.   1600 miles

3. How far is it from St. Paul to Chicago to Oklahoma City?
   - A.   800 miles
   - B.   900 miles
   - C.   1000 miles
   - D.   1200 miles

4. How far is it from Los Angeles to Dallas to Jacksonville?
   - A.   1100 miles
   - B.   1200 miles
   - C.   1500 miles
   - D.   1600 miles
   - E.   1900 miles
   - F.   2000 miles

GO ON TO THE NEXT PAGE

Fig. A.2 Examples of multiple-choice items requiring map reading and comprehension.

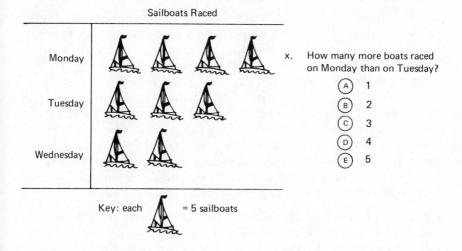

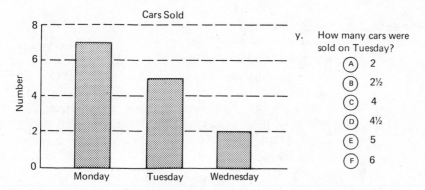

Fig. A.3 Examples of multiple-choice items requiring the use of graphs.

to be covered, it would require a minimum of two items. When the matching item is not homogeneous, a student lacking mastery of the objectives covered by the item can respond correctly simply through the association of the verbal content.

The matching item is usually structured so that the letter or number designations of the responses are matched to the premises. (See the example items which follow later in the discussion.) However, the student must have clear directions as to how the match is indicated and must also know whether or not a single response can be used more than once. Generally, it is recommended that the numbers of responses and premises be unequal, and that a student be instructed that a response may be used one or more times, or it may not be used at all.

The responses usually make up the column with the shorter entries. Responses consist of at most short phrases, and they are commonly arranged in some systematic order, such as alphabetical or, in the case of dates, chronological. The responses should be grammatically consistent. We would not have one plural response among singulars. It would be poor item construction to have one verb among noun responses and have one premise which requires a verb response.

The optimum length for matching items is between 5 to 8 premises per item with occasional longer items, but the upper limit of the range is usually set at 12. Longer items require too many comparisons, and the task becomes tedious and time consuming. Shorter items also enhance the homogeneity of the content.

Examples of matching items. With this background on constructing matching items, consider the following example of a matching item taken from social studies. This item is appropriate for lower intermediate level aged students.

Directions: Under Column A are listed characteristics or descriptions of cities in the United States. Under Column B are listed names of United States cities. Place the letter of the appropriate city name in the blank to the left of the description of Column A. You may use a city name from Column B more than once, and not all of the names will be used.

Column A	Column B
____ A city in the heart of the wheat belt	A. Albany
	B. Birmingham
____ Largest city in the Northwest	C. Chicago
	D. Denver
____ Capital of New York State	E. Detroit
	F. Kansas City
____ Great Southern steel center	G. New York
	H. Portland
____ Largest city in Rocky Mountain region	I. Salt Lake City
	J. Seattle
____ The automobile city	K. Spokane
____ A Lake Michigan seaport	
____ Largest city in Oregon	

Note that there are eight premises and eleven responses. In this item no response is used more than once. The content of the item is homogeneous with respect to cities, but not geography. This may cause a weakness for testing certain knowledge. For example, a student might not know that Portland is Oregon's largest city, but could respond correctly by recognizing Portland as the only Oregon city listed.

The following matching item is taken from a science test. The item is not as clearly homogeneous as the previous one since the response list consists of terms related to a variety of science concepts. This particular item has an equal number of premises and responses, a characteristic not usually suggested. However, it is certainly an adequate, illustrative item.

```
Directions: List A contains events that happen in
            everyday life. List B contains words or
            phrases that are scientific descriptions
            of the events in List A. Write the letter
            of the word or phrase in List B next to
            the event it describes in List A.
            List A                  List B
_____ 1. The sun rises.         A. Expansion
_____ 2. Clothes dry.           B. Condensation
_____ 3. Wood burns.            C. Revolution of the earth
_____ 4. Spring follows         D. Precipitation
         winter.
_____ 5. Clouds form.           E. Rotation of the earth
_____ 6. Rain falls.            F. Oxidation
_____ 7. Water freezes.         G. Germination
_____ 8. Seeds sprout.          H. Evaporation
```

The responses of List B are not arranged in any systematic order, but that is of little concern since the responses are readily comprehended by the examinee. However, the item would be improved if (1) the responses were listed in alphabetical order and (2) an additional one to three responses were added to List B.

Identifying plausible responses. It is relatively easy to maintain homogenous content in a matching item by limiting the scope of the item. Probably the most difficult part of constructing matching items is identifying responses which are plausible for every premise. In the first example item, this characteristic is at least technically met since cities only are involved. However, irrelevant clues may be introduced and items should be carefully scrutinized.

Short-Answer Items

Short-answer items consist of items for which the student supplies an answer rather than selecting a response from a given set of responses. The items generally take one of three forms: question, association, or completion. Each form will be illustrated with items actually constructed by elementary school teachers.

Question form. The question form is exactly what the name implies, a question posed in the item. Items in mathematics lend themselves readily to this form. For example:

> Last year Mr. Jones drove his car 14,112 miles. If he averaged 48 miles per hour, how many hours did he spend in his car last year?
>
> Answer: ——————— hours.

The above item is straightforward and there is no doubt about what form the answer is to take. Usually the direct question is easier to phrase than an incomplete statement type item which requires completion. If there is any question about matters such as the degree of accuracy expected in the answer, this should be specified for the student.

Association form. The association form is one in which the student is given a set of words or phrases and is required to supply an association with each of the words or phrases in the set. The student is given the basis of the association indicating the type of response that is expected. The first example matching item used in the preceding section can partially be converted to a short-answer association item as follows:

> Before each descriptive phrase, write the name of the United States *city* that fits the phrase:
>
> ——————————————— Largest city in the Northwest
> ——————————————— Capital of New York State
> ——————————————— The automobile city
> ——————————————— Largest city in Oregon

Note that parts of the matching item were not used, those parts that do not have unique answers. In this format it is generally more efficient to use only items that have unique answers.

Completion form. The completion form is probably the least popular of the short-answer item. With this form a statement with one or more missing words is presented and the student is to supply the missing words. Ambiguous phrasing can easily enter into a completion item. For example, an item such as:

John F. Kennedy was a ——————— .

does not provide enough direction for the student to realize what kind of response is expected. There are any number of correct responses. A better phrasing of the item would be:

The political party to which John F. Kennedy belonged was the ——— ——— party.

When preparing completion items only important words should be omitted and preferably the blanks should come near the end of the statement. Excessive numbers of blanks should be avoided because they tend to obscure the meaning of the item. The item without the answers must retain adequate structure and meaning so the student can respond in an unambiguous way.

Short-answer items do require the students to provide their own responses rather than simply select a response as with the other objective-type items discussed earlier. In this sense short-answer items are similar to essay items. Short-answer items can be effectively used to measure knowledge of facts, definitions, technical terms and the like. In mathematics they can be used to test limited computation and problem interpretation.

ESSAY ITEMS

There are two major characteristics that distinguish essay items from objective items and these are the length and type of anticipated response. With objective items a very short response, often in the form of a check mark of some sort, is required. With an essay item the response is much longer, consisting of up to several paragraphs of narrative produced by the student. The response basically consists of an "essay" and hence the name. With objective items the student often is required to select a response from two or more alternatives provided. With essay items the student is required to structure the response.

Essay Items and Objectives

One of the reasons commonly given for the use of essay items is that essay items, properly constructed, measure learning outcomes of objectives in the higher levels of the taxonomy of instructional objectives. By higher levels are meant analysis, synthesis, and evaluation outcomes in contrast to the lower levels of knowledge, comprehension, and application.

The fact that an item is an essay item does in no way ensure that the item is measuring a higher level learning outcome. In fact, one of the most common misuses of essay items is using them to measure lower level, even knowledge, outcomes and limiting them to these levels. These kinds of outcomes can more efficiently be measured by objective items. Essay items should not consist of defining terms or requiring only recall behavior of the students. For example, the item:

> List the major methods of transportation used in the large urban areas of the United States.

is an item that involves no more than factual recall. It should not appear as an essay item.

If essay items are to measure higher order learning outcomes, the student behavior when responding to such items must reflect these outcomes. Synthesis behavior is not obtained by having students identify, label, or define. Assuming the instructional objectives to be well stated, if essay items are called for, the kinds of student behaviors required should be inferred from the objectives. A single essay item would likely call forth more than one type of student behavior or skill.

Keeping with the transportation theme introduced in the item above, an essay item might consist of:

> Design and diagram (on the accompanying map) the train, bus, and auto transportation systems for an urban area of 200,000 population. Contrast the transportation needed and used between Individual A who lives and works downtown, and Individual B who lives in a suburban area five miles from the nearest bus or train stop and who works downtown. Consider points such as time spent in transportation, cost, and convenience.

In responding to this item the student would be required to synthesize the knowledge of land transportation. The student would need to organize the systems and develop a balance between them. The latter part of the item requires some evaluation of the transportation needs and uses of the two individuals.

It should not be inferred that essay items are never to measure lower level learning outcomes. Some lower level outcomes may be necessary as prerequisites of higher level outcomes, even in the same item. But essay items should not be limited to, nor should their major emphasis be on, student behaviors that reflect lower level learning outcomes.

Advantages of Essay Items

One advantage of the essay item has already been discussed, that is, its potential for measuring higher level learning outcomes. Essay items provide the student an opportunity to organize, analyze, and synthesize ideas. They also provide an opportunity for developing the student's own ideas and writing them in an organized manner. These kinds of behaviors provide an excellent learning experience, not usually developed to the same extent when using objective items.

The essay item is commonly viewed, primarily on a logical basis, as a device for measuring and improving a student's writing skills and skills in self-expression. Objective items basically do not provide a medium through which the student can demonstrate self-expression. The response to an essay item can be evaluated with respect to English usage, sentence structure, spelling, and penmanship. Whenever the response is so evaluated, the student should be aware of it, and the criteria for evaluation should be identified.

Although good essay items are not easy to prepare, they tend to be more easily prepared than good objective items. The development of plausible distractors, which can be difficult and time consuming when preparing objective items, is not required for essay items. Generally, it takes approximately the same amount of time to construct a good essay item as an objective item. The number of essay items required for a specified testing time is much less than the number of objective items for the same period. Hence, the preparation time is reduced when preparing items for a specified testing time.

Finally, there is a subtle advantage that the use of essay items has for the instructional process. If all testing is to be done by objective items, the teachers may either consciously or unconsciously bias their teaching in a certain direction. This bias will, of course, be reflected in the learning experiences of the students. If this were the case, the development of certain student skills might well suffer if not be neglected altogether.

Disadvantages of Essay Items

Essay items and essay examinations have been widely criticized over the past several decades.* The disadvantages of essay tests deal with the scoring; that is, essay tests tend to be unreliable and costly in scorer time. Lack of objectivity in scoring has always been a deter-

---

* See, for example, W. Coffman 1971, Essay examination. In R. Thorndike (ed.), *Educational measurement*. Washington, D. C.: American Council on Education.

rent of essay items, and without specific scoring directions, there tends to be considerable lack of agreement among competent scorers or even among the same scorer on two separate occasions. There are procedures that tend to enhance objectivity, but it is very difficult to eliminate subjectivity from the scoring of essay items.

Irrelevant factors tend to influence the scores given essay questions. These factors have nothing to do with the content being tested. An example of such a factor would be penmanship influencing the score when the item has nothing to do with penmanship. The scores may also be influenced by the order in which the papers are read. There is a tendency to score the earlier papers higher.

A serious limitation of an essay exam is its limited content sampling. With poor content sampling goes low content validity. Advocates of the essay exam could argue that they are not interested in testing for knowledge with essay items, but knowledge is a prerequisite for demonstrating higher order, cognitive outcomes. In this sense the essay item tends to overemphasize the importance of how to say something and neglects the importance of knowing what to say.

Improving Essay Items

Although the limitations of essay items and essay tests are very real, there are procedures that can be used to improve the items. These procedures are directed primarily toward enhancing the objectivity of scoring and improving the reliability of the test in which the items appear.

Restricting the item and its response. Essay items used at the elementary school level should require restricted rather than extended responses. It is somewhat difficult to distinguish items as requiring a restricted or extended response since the extent of response is basically a continuum. But with elementary age students the length of response should tend toward the restricted end of the continuum. If the item establishes a definite and limited framework within which the student responds, it not only limits the response but also enhances the objectivity of scoring. Very general questions leave the student at a loss on how to respond, and correspondingly the teacher will have difficulty in scoring the responses.

There are any number of ways in which a framework can be established for the response to an item. Consider the development of the following item which as initially stated is too general.

Original item: Describe the development of the highway system in the United States.

Why is this item too general? For one thing, it provides no limits to a very extended topic. No periods of development are indicated. Is the student to begin with the first highway and continue through the most recent interstate completion? No subset of the highway system is indicated. Are all kinds of highways to be discussed? These are the kinds of points for which the item provides no direction.

In an attempt to restrict the item we might provide limits as follows:

Item revision 1: Describe the development of the interstate highway system in the United States from 1955 to the present.

This revision of the item is an improvement over the original in that it indicates both a definite part of the highway system and a period in time of its development.

The item directs the student to one activity only, namely "describe." This may be adequate, but in the context of the item it may be somewhat vague and general. In any event, it would be helpful to provide additional or substitute words which are more descriptive of what the student is to do.

Item revision 2: Diagram the development of the interstate highway system in the United States from 1955 to the present. Label all parts of the diagram indicating the time of completion of major segments. Explain why the major segments were placed where they are.

If oral directions are provided, the teacher might define more specifically what is meant by "explain." Especially with younger children words such as contrast, distinguish, and generalize require additional definition in the context of the specific item. Whatever the level of the children, the vocabulary of the item should be words that they understand. For the item above it would be well to provide a blank map of the United States for student use in responding.

In restricting or limiting an essay item, more specific verbs tend to be used, the verbs reflecting the student behaviors. A single item would likely include two or more student behaviors. This not only has the effect of restricting the item and the response, but it also increases the sampling of student behaviors.

Directing the student to the desired response. As an essay item is developed, the teacher should attempt to define the students' task as much as possible and still require them to select, organize, and express their ideas. Restricting the item to some extent provides direction, but the item must require the kind of student behavior that was intended. It is relatively easy to phrase items that do not require the student behavior that the teacher infers. For example, phrasing items such as, "What do you think of . . ." clearly calls for an opinion from the student, and in this form does not require analysis, synthesis, etc., on the part of the student. An erroneous phrasing of an item is, "Write all you know about. . . ." The response to an item so phrased can easily be limited to simple recall. Another serious deficiency of an item so phrased is that it can be graded only as 100 percent correct. Suppose the student responds by writing, "I don't know anything about. . . ." This is a correct response to the directions of the item. So, the phrasing of essay items should be carefully reviewed by the unit staff to make certain the intended student behaviors are required by the item.

More items with shorter responses. With elementary school age students, it is best to use greater numbers of essay items that require shorter responses rather than just a few items requiring longer responses. Seldom should a response require more than one-half page, say, not over 150 handwritten words. Length of response can vary with the cognitive maturity of the students.

Evaluating the response. The response to an essay item must be scored and evaluated by at least one teacher and, if time permits, it may be desirable to have more than one teacher score the item. However, if the criteria by which the item is to be scored are well defined, it is not necessary to have multiple scores.

Prior to administering an item, external factors such as handwriting, spelling, etc., that will be considered in evaluating the response should be identified. The student should be told prior to responding what factors are going to be considered and their relative importance, if different weights will be used in the scoring of the response.

The major substantive points that are to be included in the response should be identified prior to scoring responses. There may be a tendency to avoid this consideration and wait until some responses are available. This is a serious mistake because the scorer may be somewhat vague about what should be included in the response. Oversights can easily occur. Also, without a scoring guide, scoring tends to become relative as more and more responses are read. If the measurement is criterion-referenced, this is like trying to score without a criterion.

The identification of major substantive points tends to lessen scorer bias and also tends to enhance consistency of scoring when two or more scorers are used.

Careful as the teachers may be in constructing an item and directing the student to the response, there are times when students come up with responses that may be correct but not as the teacher intended. For example, the solution to a science problem might be arrived at through a "nonscientific" manner. How will the response to such an item be scored? If a correct solution only is required, the response must be considered correct. However, if the purpose of the item is to have the student demonstrate a scientific solution, scoring a nonscientific solution as correct would not be acceptable. The kinds of responses considered acceptable should be identified when developing the scoring. The student should also be informed of the kinds of acceptable responses.

There are some "procedural" steps that can be taken to enhance the objectivity of scoring essay items, at least objectivity and consistency across the student responses. One such step is to score the papers anonymously. That is, avoid identifying the student who made the response until after it is scored. The mechanics of doing this may be somewhat cumbersome and the student's handwriting may be recognized anyway.

If two or more essay items appear on a test it is well to score all the responses to one item rather than score all the items on a single test before going on to the next test paper. It is less confusing to the individual scoring the items if concentration is on one item only at a time. The scoring criteria are more likely to remain consistent across the responses to the item. Also, by scoring all responses to one item, there is less likelihood of a poor (or good) response to an item influencing the scoring of responses to other items. If a student does a poor job of responding to the first essay item, this could influence the score if responses to other items are read immediately.

A reader may inadvertently shift criteria as the reading of responses progresses. Therefore, it is good practice to reorder the test papers after reading the responses to an item and before reading those of the next item. In this way a student's responses are not always read in the same position. Reordering papers tends to lessen the chances of a student's score being at least in part a function of where the test paper is located in the pile of test papers.

Avoid Optional Essay Items on a Test

In an attempt to increase the content sampling of essay items, there may be a tendency to provide more items and allow the student to respond to a limited number that are self-selected. Generally, this practice is undesirable for three major reasons.

1. It is difficult to construct items of equal difficulty.
2. Students do not have the ability to select those questions upon which they will be able to do best.
3. Good students may be penalized because they are challenged by the more difficult and complex items.*

Because of reasons one and three above, it is very difficult to establish consistent scoring when optional items are provided.

The matter of providing optional items on a test should not be confused with having different groups or even individual students responding to different items. When programing instruction for the individual student it would not be reasonable to argue that all students should be responding to the same set of items at the same time. When testing, the items included should be determined by the objectives that the students are attempting to meet.

In summary, the preparation of good essay items depends most on providing an adequate framework for the student so that the desired student behaviors are required of the response. Teachers have a tendency not to provide enough directions and structure for the response much more so than to overstructure the item. Items should be carefully checked for vague or unfamiliar wording. Definite descriptions of what the student is expected to do should be included in the item.

---

* W. A. Mehrens and I. J .Lehmann 1973, *Measurement and evaluation in education and psychology*, New York: Holt, Rinehart, and Winston, p. 222.

Glossary

Accountability   The extent to which persons are held responsible for their task performance.

Accountability, educational   The idea that teachers and school systems may be held responsible for actual improvement in student achievement and that such improvement is measurable.

Affective domain   The area of learning or instruction pertaining to the feelings and emotions.

Affective outcomes of education   Results which involve feelings more than understandings. Likes and dislikes, satisfactions and discontents, ideals and values are some of the affective outcomes that education may develop in the individual.

Age norm   The average score on an aptitude or achievement test for students of a specific age group. Age norms are usually reported in tables showing the average scores of students in a series of different age groups.

Alternate-forms reliability   Reliability established through the correlation between scores on two equivalent forms of the test, administered to the same group of individuals.

Anecdotal method   A technique by means of which behavior and responses are recorded, as they occur.

Assessment   Application of a measurement procedure; obtaining data through measurement, does not include a judgment, therefore is nonevaluative measurement; assessment is also used by some writers as a synonym for either evaluation or measurement.

Attitude   An orientation toward or away from some object, concept, or situation; a readiness to respond in a predetermined manner to the object, concept, or situation.

Chance score   The expected score on a multiple choice or true-false test if the student had simply guessed at the correct responses.

Cognitive domain   The area of learning or instruction pertaining to attaining and using knowledge.

Cognitive outcomes of education   Results from education in the intellectual skills; not to be confused with an objective of education, which is a desired result of education.

Criterion, mastery   A standard that explicitly indicates full or complete attainment of an objective or objectives, usually in the cognitive or psychomotor domain; e.g., 90 percent correct on a 30-item test that measures attainment of three objectives in science; walking a mile in 15 minutes without stopping to rest or running. Mastery criteria are usually set when it is known or presumed that one objective, or set of objectives, must be attained fully before the next one can be undertaken successfully.

Criterion-referenced measurement (testing, assessment)   Measurement, the results of which are interpreted with respect to what the student knows or can do rather than relating the results to those of some external reference group.

Criterion, variable   A standard that implies that either (a) not all students must attain the same level of knowledge, skill, or affective outcome, or (b) that a particular lesson or unit contains several objectives, not all of which are to be attained to the same specified level. Variable criteria are generally set in connection with expressive objectives, objectives in the affective domain, and objectives in the psychomotor domain. In general, only a limited number of objectives in the skill subjects are to be attained to mastery by all students at one time during their elementary school years, and even here allowances are made for exceptional students; e.g., blind, deaf, emotionally disturbed, mentally retarded.

Constructed response test   A test for which the student must supply the response rather than selecting from given options. An essay test is a constructed response test.

Decision making   The act of making a choice among defined alternatives concerning a defined issue or problem.

***Developing Mathematical Processes* (DMP)**   A comprehensive instructional and management program in elementary mathematics that integrates arithmetic, geometry, and probability and statistics.

Diagnostic item set   A set of items that can be scored in such a way that certain patterns of incorrect responses isolate specific types of errors being made by students.

Diagnostic test   A test the results of which are used to identify or analyze a student's specific strengths and weaknesses.

Evaluation   The science of providing information for decision making—the process of delineating, obtaining, and providing useful information for judging decision alternatives.

Evaluation, formative   Evaluation of a student's learning during an instructional sequence; evaluation of instructional product activities while it is being developed; evaluation of a process while it is being conducted.

Evaluation, process   Evaluation of a process such as the instructional activities being implemented.

Evaluation, product   Evaluation of a product such as scores on a criterion test.

Evaluation, summative   Evaluation of a student's learning at the end of an instructional sequence, evaluation of a completed process.

Grade equivalent   The mean or median achievement of pupils in a given school grade on a given standardized test. Grade norm tables usually present these mean scores for several adjacent grades.

Grade equivalent score   An individual's score, usually from a standardized test, expressed as the grade level for which the score is the actual or estimated average.

Individually Guided Education (IGE)   A comprehensive form of schooling that is an alternative to the age-graded, self-contained form of schooling; it is designed to produce higher education achievements and to attain other educational objectives through providing well for differences among students in rate of learning, learning style, and other characteristics.

Individually Guided Motivation (IGM)   A program for focusing a school's efforts on motivation in accordance with instructional programming for the individual student; four motivational-instructional procedures are designed to increase children's interest in learning related to any curricular area and also to promote their self-direction.

Instructional Improvement Committee (IIC)   The organizational element of the multiunit school organization structure at the school level. It is made up of unit leaders and a parent representative. The IIC carries out many planning and evaluating functions regarding instruction previously performed by the principal or teachers independently.

Instructional program for the individual student   (1) The teaching-learning activities by which the student attains one or more instructional objectives over a short period of time (students with the same needs and readiness may have the same instructional program in a given curriculum area) (2) The combination of all the student's teaching-learning activities in the various curriculum areas for any given period of time.

Instructional Programming (for the individual student)   The process of identifying objectives, planning and carrying out a series of related activities and use of materials (learning experiences) by which a student is to attain the objectives to a stated criterion; the amount of time may or may not be specified.

Instructional Programming Model (IPM)   A seven-step model for planning, carrying out, and evaluating instructional programs for the individual students of a school. The model takes into account these conditions: that some but not all instructional objectives should be attained by all students during the elementary school; that some but not all objectives should be attained by students to a criterion of mastery, and that some, but not most, objectives are attained in a fixed and invariant sequence.

Instruction and Research (I & R) Unit   An element of the multiunit school organization typically consisting of a unit leader, three to five staff teachers, an instructional secretary, a teacher aide, and 100-150 students; the I & R Unit replaces the age-graded self-contained classroom organization for instruction. The staff of the unit is a hierarchically organized team with clearly defined job descriptions.

Internal consistency   A test possesses internal consistency if it is composed of items that all measure much the same thing and that are therefore highly intercorrelated. A measure of internal consistency provides one measure of test reliability.

Interval measurement scale   A scale which in addition to classifying and ordering also establishes equal units between points on the scale. (Also called an equal unit scale.)

Item analysis   A study to determine the difficulty and discriminating power of test item. The difficulty of an item is usually expressed as the percent of the group of examinees who failed to answer the item correctly. Its discriminating power may be expressed as a difference between the proportions of good and poor students who answered the item correctly. Applied to multiple-choice items, the counting of responses from students of high and low overall achievements reveals the effectiveness of each distracter.

Item difficulty index   Of a test item, the proportion of respondents that answered an item correctly.

Item discrimination index   A measure which can range from -1 to $+1$ inclusive and indicates how well an item separates the top and bottom extremes in a distribution of scores.

Item-generating rule   An algorithm for constructing parallel items.

Kuder-Richardson formulas   Formulas used for estimating the reliability of a test based on one administration of the test; the formulas involve the inter-item correlation.

Mean   A measure of the central tendency or the average numerical value of a set of scores. It is calculated by adding all of the scores and dividing the sum by the number of scores.

Measurement   A process of assigning numbers to an object or the members of a set.

Median   The point in a score distribution that divides it into two parts containing equal numbers of scores. If the number of scores in the distribution is odd, the median is the middle score. If the number is even, the median is a point midway between the two scores nearest the middle. The median is identical with the fifth decile or the fiftieth percentile.

Mode   In a distribution, the score of greatest frequency.

Multiunit school organization   A three-level, instructional-organizational pattern consisting of an Instruction and Research Unit; an Instructional Improvement Committee within the building; and a Systemwide Program Committee within the school district.

Nominal measurement scale   A scale which merely classifies objects or events by assigning numbers to them.

Normative group   The reference group that is the basis for interpreting the results of a norm-referenced test.

Norm-referenced measurement (testing, assessment)   Measurement conducted with the intention of interpreting the results so as to differentiate individuals or to discriminate among the individuals of some defined group.

Objective, expressive   An instructional objective stated in terms of the kind and/or number of activities to be engaged in.

Objective, instructional   A statement describing the desired results that may be expected from the particular unit or sequence of instruction.

Ordinal measurement scale   A scale which classifies and assigns rank order to whatever is being measured.

Parallel forms, of a test   Two forms of a test constructed independently but equivalent with respect to content, difficulty, etc. (Also called equivalent forms.)

Performance   Overt or readily measured behavior, as distinguished from knowledge or information not translated into action.

Positional preference   A tendency of a test constructor to consistently place the correct response in the same position when constructing an objective test; a tendency of a test taker to select responses which are in the same position.

Posttest   A test administered following some kind of treatment, or in an instructional setting, administered after the instruction has taken place.

Pretest   A test administered prior to some kind of treatment, or in an instructional setting, administered prior to instruction.

Probability   The likelihood of an event occurring expressed as a number between 0 and 1 inclusive; 0 representing no possibility of occurrence, 1 representing certainty of occurrence.

Range   A measure of variability in a distribution of scores given by the difference between the highest and lowest score in which case it is called the exclusive range. The inclusive range is the difference between the upper real limit of the highest score and the lowest real limit of the lowest score.

Rating scale   A device by which raters can record their judgment of another person (or of themselves) on the traits defined by the scale.

Ratio measurement scale   A scale that contains all the properties of an interval scale plus a nonarbitrary zero point.

Reliability, of a test or measuring instrument   The consistency of a test in measuring whatever it measures.

Split-half reliability   Reliability established by separating the items of a test into two parallel parts, correlating the scores on the two halves, and applying the Spearman-Brown formula.

Standard deviation   A measure of variability given by the square root of the average squared deviation from the mean; the positive square root of the variance of a distribution of scores.

Standard error of measurement   Conceptually, the standard deviation of an individual's distribution of test scores over a large number of test administrations; computationally, given by S.E.M. $= \sigma \sqrt{1 - r_{11}}$ where σ is the standard deviation of a distribution of test scores and r_{11} is the reliability of the test.

Standardized test   A test which is administered and scored, according to specified directions, and interpreted with respect to normative information. Such tests are generally commercially published, although all commercially published tests are not standardized.

Test   A collection of items (questions, tasks, etc.) so arranged that replies or performances can be scored and interpreted.

Test, achievement   An instrument designed to measure a student's accomplishment or proficiency related to some body of knowledge or skill, often used to measure achievement in arithmetic, chemistry, English, typing, and other subjects of study; most tests made by teachers for classroom use are achievement tests.

Test, diagnostic   An instrument designed to reveal specific weaknesses or failures to learn in some subject of study such as reading or arithmetic. In a diagnostic test the main interest is in scores on individual items or on small groups of highly similar items.

Test, mastery   An instrument not intended to indicate how much a student has achieved relative to other students, but only whether or not the student has achieved enough to satisfy the minimum requirements of the teacher or the examining agency.

Test-retest reliability   Reliability established through the correlation between scores on two separate administrations of the test to the same group of individuals.

Unobtrusive measure   Measurements taken without the student's awareness.

Usability of a test   Factors related to a test such as ease of scoring, ease of administration, cost and availability, that determine the practical considerations in selecting a test.

Validity   The extent to which a test of measuring instrument meets the purpose for which it is intended, or the extent to which it measures what it purports to measure.

Validity, concurrent   Criterion-related validity for which the criterion is some present performance.

Validity, content   Validity based on the extent to which the test adequately samples the domain of possible items.

Validity, criterion-related   Validity established by how well the test score is a predictor of some criterion which is usually performance on another test or on some measurable task.

Validity, predictive   Criterion-related validity for which the criterion is some future performance.

Variance   A measure of variability given by the average squared deviations from the mean; the square of the standard deviation.

Wisconsin Design for Reading Skill Development (WDRSD)   A reading program which describes six areas of reading skills and related behavioral and expressive objectives; it provides machine-scorable, criterion-referenced tests for assessing student attainment of behavioral and expressive objectives; it also provides the means for managing objective-based instruction in reading.

Work sample   A nontest product of student learning, such as a handwriting sample, a science project, or a written report.

Indexes

Author Index

Subject Index